Revelation

THE COMPLETE PORTRAIT OF THE MESSIAH

Volume 10

Other volumes in The Complete Portrait of the Messiah series

Volume 1: *The Pentateuch*
Volume 2: *The Gospels*
Volume 3: *The Historical Books*
Volume 4: *Acts*
Volume 5: *The Wisdom Books*
Volume 6: *Paul's Letters*
Volume 7: *The Major Prophets*
Volume 8: *General Letters*
Volume 9: *The Minor Prophets*
Volume 10: *Revelation*

Also available from Time to Revive and Laura Kim Martin

reviveDAILY: A Devotional Journey from Genesis to Revelation, Year 1
reviveDAILY: A Devotional Journey from Genesis to Revelation, Year 2

Revelation

THE COMPLETE PORTRAIT OF THE MESSIAH

Volume 10

Kyle Lance Martin

Time to Revive and reviveSCHOOL

time to
revive
Richardson, Texas

Revelation

Published in conjunction with
Iron Stream Media
100 Missionary Ridge
Birmingham, AL 35242
IronStreamMedia.com

Copyright © 2024 by Time to Revive

Iron Stream Media serves its authors as they express their views, which may not
express the views of the publisher.

Library of Congress Control Number: 2024907113

978-1-63204-113-5 (hardback)
978-1-63204-115-9 (eBook)

1 2 3 4 5—28 27 26 25 24

DEDICATION

Greetings friends and colaborers of the Lord Jesus Christ!

I am writing to you with an excitement that is beyond words. For I would like to dedicate this book to individuals like yourselves whose desire to grow closer to Jesus and go deeper in the Word of God brings such JOY to my heart. And my prayer for each one of you is that the Holy Spirit will reveal more of Himself to you in this in-depth time of studying the Word of God daily. Jesus said, "Blessed are those who hunger and thirst for righteousness, for they will be satisfied" (Matthew 5:6 NASB). So as you embark on this journey of studying each book of the Bible, may you experience a freshness and a fulfillment that can only come from the Spirit of God. You will have days that you won't want to wake up early and read. There will be moments when life throws you a situation that delays your personal devotional time with Him. But please press in and allow the Holy Spirit to strengthen your every step. This will allow you to exercise your faith muscles and walk out what you are learning in this. From my experience, obedience will bring education to life!

It will be quite a strenuous commitment, yet it's a part of an intentional strategy to equip the saints for His return. And your participation with revive-SCHOOL is a unique part of this preparation.

May the Lord receive all the glory, honor, and fame in this pursuit of righteousness.

Praying,
Dr. Kyle Lance Martin

CONTENTS

reviveSCHOOL History and Introduction

In January of 2015, our ministry, Time to Revive, was invited from our home base in Richardson, Texas, to Goshen, Indiana, to help equip the local church to learn how to go out and share the gospel in their community. We called it reviveINDIANA. During this frigid first trip in January, our intention was to help facilitate a week of prayer and outreach as a form of training, which we hoped would lead to an intentional week of outreach later that year. Little did we know that God had other plans.

The week of prayer and outreach started with about 450 people from various churches in the community and, to our surprise, quickly swelled to over 3,000. And by the end of that first week, the Holy Spirit confirmed to a group of us, including local pastors, that the Time to Revive team should stay for 52 straight days! Imagine the phone calls we had to make to our spouses telling them we were going to stay a "little" longer.

Over the course of these seven weeks, the local church witnessed God move in mighty ways, and each person involved could tell you miraculous testimonies of how they witnessed, firsthand, how God was moving. The 52 days culminated on March 4 of that year where an estimated 10,000 people showed up to brave the cold temperatures and go out and share the love of Jesus Christ.

All the while, word of this was spreading throughout the state, and it led to the Time to Revive team being invited to seven different cities in Indiana over the course of the next seven months. We continued to witness the local body of believers in these various communities encouraged and equipped to continue to take out their faith and share with others. The gospel wasn't intended to stay only in the church building. Jesus commissioned each one of us to go and make disciples in our own Jerusalem, Judea, and Samaria and to the ends of the earth.

Back in Goshen, the local body continued to go out regularly after those initial 52 days while keeping track of the days since that first amazing week. A couple of years later in 2017, the local believers invited our team to celebrate their 1,000th day of outreach in their community. It was during that time when a local man shared with us a dream he had, which led us to start a two-year Bible study in the community. Similar to the Apostle Paul as he taught 12 disciples in Ephesus to study the Word of God on a daily basis, Time to Revive's desire was to also provide in-depth teaching that would focus on where the Messiah is found in every book of the Bible from Genesis to Revelation. We knew this would deepen their commitment to sharing the gospel as well as deepen their relationship with the Lord and with those whom they were discipling.

> But when some became hardened and would not believe, slandering the Way in front of the crowd, he withdrew from them and met separately with the disciples, conducting discussions every day in the lecture hall of Tyrannus. —Acts 19:9

This local Bible study started with 12 men who signed up and committed to study the Word of God in a barn on a county road in Goshen, Indiana. And on January 1, 2018, we launched reviveSCHOOL with 54 men in this initial group. They studied the Scriptures daily, using the online resources, then gathered in the barn to discuss them in person. Each student studied the Bible daily using these resources:

- a Scripture reading plan to stay on track,
- a 29-minute teaching video (by Kyle Lance Martin, Indiana pastors, and TTR teachers),
- a devotion (written by Laura Kim Martin),
- reading guide questions to help facilitate discussion and critical thinking,
- lesson plans to summarize the daily teaching, and
- a painting of each book of the Bible by Mindi Oaten.

Upon the completion of the two-year study in the Word, Time to Revive celebrated over 200 students who had joined reviveSCHOOL with a graduation ceremony in January 2020. Plans were made for these individuals to take the Word and launch reviveSCHOOL groups not only in the United States but also throughout various nations. However, with worldwide travel restrictions due to the COVID-19 pandemic, this travel didn't happen. Thankfully, God had another plan, His plan was "above and beyond" all that Time to Revive could ask or think of (Ephesians 3:20–21).

With all the reviveSCHOOL materials already available online, the Holy Spirit spread the word to pastors and leaders of nations all throughout the world. Believers were hungry for biblically sound teaching and resources to grow closer to the Lord. As exemplified in Acts 19 with Paul and the disciples, and all the people of Asia, the Word of God through reviveSCHOOL truly spread—from a barn in Indiana to the nations.

> And this went on for two years, so that all the inhabitants of Asia, both Jews and Greeks, heard the message about the Lord. —Acts 19:10

By God's grace, reviveSCHOOL has become an outlet for individuals to gain fresh insight into the Messiah all throughout the Scriptures, as well as to develop an understanding of the role of Israel from a biblical perspective.

I am humbled and honored that you would select reviveSCHOOL for your learning. When we started with 12 guys in a Bible study, we had no idea that reviveSCHOOL would be as far reaching as it has become. Our team would delight in knowing that you are studying the Word of God and using the resources with reviveSCHOOL. We pray that through these resources you will grow closer to the Lord and that you are inspired to walk out the plans that God has for your life by exposing others to the love of Christ.

To God be the glory!
Dr. Kyle Lance Martin

For further information about how to sign up for this two-year study in the Word of God or if you would like to launch a reviveSCHOOL group in your community, state/province, or country, please go online to www.reviveSCHOOL.org.

How to Use this Bible Study Series

The *Complete Portrait of the Messiah* Bible study series contains multiple components for each lesson. These components work together to provide an in-depth study of how Jesus is revealed throughout the whole of Scripture. Below is a description of each component and how you can use each one to maximize your study experience.

Teaching Notes and Video Lessons
The teaching notes summarize the main points of each video lesson and include a QR code to access the video teaching. If you have access to the internet via your phone, you can scan the QR code to watch the video lesson.*

The Daily Word Devotional
Dig deeper into personal application for each lesson through *The Daily Word* devotional. This day-by-day devotional encourages you with thoughts for application and further Scripture readings.

Reading Guide Questions
These questions will guide you into a more detailed exploration of each lesson's content. Examine the concepts of the daily Scripture readings in more detail.

The Bible Art Collection
This Bible study series is augmented by a one-of-a-kind, especially inspired series of original artwork created by artist Mindi Oaten. These 66 acrylic paintings creatively depict the revelation of Christ in each book of the Bible. Viewing each of these original art pieces will inspire your understanding and further enrich your understanding of Jesus throughout all of the Scriptures. These can be found at https://www.mindioaten.com/pages/mindi-oaten-art-bible-art-collection or https://www.reviveschool.org/

❦

About the Cover

Revelation
"The Beginning and the End"

Artist Notes: Mindi Oaten

There were so many ways I could have painted Revelation. After asking the Lord, He simply showed me a picture of Him holding out a wedding bouquet from the Garden of Eden. The image was that simple. I heard Him clearly say He is calling His Bride forth. Those who know Him will be the ones who come to the wedding. "Look, I am coming quickly!" (Revelation 22:7a). He is coming back to restore His Kingdom. After sketching what I was seeing, I read the end of Revelation, and chapter 22 was what I saw, the restoration of Eden. The last painting of this collection inspires reflection on the continuity of God's grace in Christ from Genesis to Revelation. The full fragrance of the Garden of Eden, from beginning to end, has always been with Christ, as He holds out the bouquet to His Bride, the saints of all the ages.

Jesus Holding Bouquet:

"Look, I am coming quickly! The one who keeps the prophetic words of this book is blessed." (Revelation 22:7)

"Look! I am coming quickly, and My reward is with Me to repay each person according to what he has done." (Revelation 22:12)

"Both the Spirit and the bride say, 'Come!' Anyone who hears should say, 'Come!' And the one who is thirsty should come. Whoever desires should take the living water as a gift." (Revelation 22:17)

I painted Jesus holding a bouquet of flowers and fruit from the Garden, reminiscent of a wedding bouquet. The action I saw in my vision was Jesus holding it out to me. It felt like a reward at the finish line, one that I had to reach for to receive those flowers. Jesus offers us the "garden of life." Are we ready and positioned to receive it? Do we know Him personally to marry Him? Those were questions I felt the Spirit speaking to my heart. It is all about knowing the Lord intimately in right relationship with Him.

Fruits/Crops:

"Then he showed me the river of living water, sparkling like crystal, flowing from the throne of God and of the Lamb down the middle of the broad street of the city. The tree of life was on both sides of the river, bearing 12 kinds of fruit, producing its fruit every month. The leaves of the tree are for healing the nations, and there will no longer be any curse. The throne of God and of the Lamb will be in the city, and His slaves will serve Him." (Revelation 22:1–3)

I painted twelve fruits and grains in the bouquet to represent the twelve crops of fruit from the tree of life mentioned in the verse above.

Light Aqua Background with Light:

"Night will no longer exist, and people will not need lamplight or sunlight, because the Lord God will give them light. And they will reign forever and ever." (Revelation 22:5)

For the background of this painting, I used the same aqua color I used in Genesis, only adding more white to make it "light" and give the effect of brightness, no more night or darkness. Jesus is the Light. There is no more darkness when He returns for His bride, the church.

Blue Butterfly:

I couldn't resist adding one more butterfly! I chose to paint it blue for the last butterfly of the series. This represents the Holy Spirit, the crystal water flowing from the throne, and the everlasting life we have in Christ Jesus. It's the ultimate rebirth and transformation in the New Jerusalem.

Broken Seal:

"I also saw a mighty angel proclaiming in a loud voice, 'Who is worthy to open the scroll and break its seals?'" (Revelation 5:2)

"Then one of the elders said to me, 'Stop crying. Look! The Lion from the tribe of Judah, the Root of David, has been victorious so that He may open the scroll and its seven seals.'" (Revelation 5:5)

Jesus is the only one qualified to open the seals. Because of Christ's willingness to give His life for all mankind, as the unblemished Lamb, Jesus shed His blood as the ultimate sacrifice at the cross. This alone makes Him worthy to open the scroll and the seals. He is victorious!

Red Ribbon:

"And they sang a new song:

> You are worthy to take the scroll
> and to open its seals,
> because You were slaughtered,
> and You redeemed people
> for God by Your blood
> from every tribe and language
> and people and nation.
> You made them a kingdom
> and priests to our God,
> and they will reign on the earth."
> (Revelation 5:9–10)

As I have often painted throughout this series, I included the red ribbon tied around the garden bouquet to symbolize the gift of the blood of the Lamb, shed for our freedom from sin and death.

Garden Flowers: the Bride's Bouquet—Restoration

I knew I wanted to bookend Revelation (as in Genesis) with the flowers to bring the garden flowers that were sprinkled throughout the entire project to completion. At first, my natural thoughts were to paint the garden coming down from heaven, but Jesus showed me something different that I AM is handing us the Garden.

*In reviveSCHOOL, the theme word for Jesus in Revelation is I AM.

Lesson 1: Revelation 1

I AM: John's Vision of the Risen Lord

Teaching Notes

Intro

We've spent almost two years moving through the Bible in our quest to see the Messiah in every book. In Matthew 5:17, Jesus said, "Don't assume that I came to destroy the Law or the Prophets. I did not come to destroy but to fulfill." We've seen Jesus in every book of the Bible as He came to fulfill each. As we move into the book of Revelation, we have the chance to see everything we've already studied connect together. Our phrase for the Messiah in the book of Revelation is *I AM*. Revelation 1:8 says, "'I am the Alpha and the Omega,' says the Lord God, 'the One who is, who was, and who is coming, the Almighty.'" Jesus tied Himself to the Lord (Exodus 3:14).

The title of the book is Revelation, not Revelations. It's one continual revelation of Christ. MacArthur defines revelation as "'an uncovering,' 'an unveiling,' or 'a disclosure.'"[1] The unveiling in Revelation is Christ. I am convinced that the reason we don't understand the book of Revelation is because we don't understand the other 65 books of the Bible in context. MacArthur explains the unveilings that are found in Revelation as "the unveiling of spiritual truth, the revealing of the sons of God, Christ's Incarnation, and His glorious appearing at His Second Coming."[2] He continues: "In each of its uses, revelation refers to something or someone, once hidden, becoming visible. What this book reveals or unveils is Jesus Christ in glory."[3] Jesus was hidden from the Jews, but He will be revealed to them in His second coming.

The author is the Apostle John, who also wrote the Gospel of John and 1, 2, and 3 John. John identified himself as the author, and the early church fathers Justin Martyr, Irenaeus, Clement of Alexandria, and Tertullian also support John's authorship.[4] "Many of the book's original readers were still alive

---

[1] John MacArthur, *The MacArthur Bible Commentary* (Nashville: Thomas Nelson, 2005), 1989.

[2] MacArthur, 1989.

[3] MacArthur, 1989.

[4] MacArthur, 1989.

during the lifetimes of Justin Martyr and Irenaeus—both of who held to apostolic authorship." While there are some differences in John's style of writing between his Gospel and the book of Revelation, there are similarities as well. Both books refer to Jesus as "the Word," and both books "translate Zechariah 12:10 differently from the Septuagint, but in agreement with each other."[5]

Scholars are not in agreement as to when the book was written. MacArthur suggests it was written between AD 94–96, around the end of Emperor Domitian's rule (AD 81–96). Because of spiritual decline experienced by the seven churches (Revelation 2—3), the book probably couldn't have been written earlier than that. During the 60s, the churches were strong. MacArthur explains, "The brief time between Paul's ministry there and the end of Nero's reign was too short for such a dramatic decline to have occurred. The longer time gap also explains the rise of the heretical sect known as the Nicolaitans, who are not mentioned in Paul's letters, not even to one or more of these same churches."[6]

John was the only apostle still alive in the beginning of the book. John was old at this time and had been exiled to the island of Patmos for his faithful preaching of Christ. While there, John received a series of revelations that presented the history of the world to come. At the time he was arrested, John was still ministering in Ephesus. This background helps explain John's vision of the coming persecution of the church and the hope that the *I AM* would return.[7]

The book of Revelation is intimidating because the language is prophetic. Themes include theological information about angels and the end times, as well as "the final political setup of the world; the last battle of human history; the career and ultimate defeat of Antichrist; Christ's 1,000-year earthly kingdom; the glories of heaven and the eternal state; and the final state of the wicked and the righteous."[8]

MacArthur outlines four approaches to interpreting Revelation: (1) the preterist approach looks at Revelation as a description of the historical events of time without looking to the future; (2) the historicist approach sees Revelation as a picture of the history of the church through symbolism; (3) the idealist approach sees Revelation as the cosmic battle between good and evil; and (4) the futurist approach understands chapters 6—22 as being about the future and symbolically explain what is to come.[9] MacArthur points out that only the fourth view "does justice to Revelation's claim to be prophecy and interprets the book by the same grammatical-historical method as chapters 1—3 and the rest of Scripture."[10]

---

[5] MacArthur, 1989.

[6] MacArthur, 1989–90.

[7] MacArthur, 1990.

[8] MacArthur, 1990–91.

[9] MacArthur, 1991.

[10] MacArthur, 1991.

Teaching

Revelation 1:1–8: "Revelation reveals [Christ] in His exaltation: (1) in blazing glory (vv. 7–20); (2) over His church, as its Lord (chs. 2, 3); (3) in His Second Coming, as He takes back the earth from the usurper, Satan, and establishes His kingdom (chs. 4–20); and (4) as He lights up the eternal state (chs. 21, 22)."[11] John was told to testify about what he saw, as God gave the revelation to Jesus, and then Jesus shared it with John, through an angel (vv. 1–2). There are seven "beatitudes" in Revelation (1:3; 14:13; 16:15; 19:9; 20:6; 22:7, 14) to prepare us for the end times. Wiersbe points out, "God promised a special blessing to the one who would read the book and obey its message."[12] (v. 3)

The book was addressed to the seven churches in Asia: Ephesus, Smyrna, Pergamum, Thyatira, Sardis, Philadelphia, and Laodicea (v. 4). The phrase "seven spirits" could be referencing Isaiah 11:2 and the "sevenfold ministry of the Holy Spirit," or the seven lampstands in Zechariah 4:1–10.[13] Christ is God's firstborn who has risen from the dead (v. 5), and the glory and dominion are His forever (v. 6). Verse 7 refers to Jesus' second coming on a cloud of glory (the Shekinah glory from the Old Testament), not to the rapture because everyone will see it. Those who pierced Him (the Jews) will see this. God is the supreme, eternal God (v. 8).

Revelation 1:9–20: These verses portray an incredibly beautiful picture of Christ through John's vision. John was in the presence of the Spirit of the Lord and heard a voice like a trumpet. He was told to write the visions down and send them to the churches in Asia. The seven lampstands (v. 12) probably refer to the church, and Christ is dressed as the High Priest in a robe with a gold sash (v. 13). His hair was white (Daniel 7), and His eyes were like a fiery flame for a penetrating look into the church (v. 14). The voice changed to the sound of cascading waters (v. 15). Judgment is portrayed in verse 15, and Christ was seen holding seven stars in His hand (v. 16). John responded by falling at Jesus' feet like a dead man (v. 17). Jesus identified Himself as *I AM*, the First and the Last, the Living One who was dead but now lives forever (v. 18). There will be nothing to fear because God will send His angel messengers (the seven stars) to the seven churches (the seven lampstands) (vv. 19–20).

Closing

This sets the stage for the rest of the book of Revelation.

---

[11] MacArthur, 1992.

[12] Warren W. Wiersbe, *The Wiersbe Bible Commentary: New Testament* (Colorado Springs: David C. Cook, 2007), 567.

[13] MacArthur, 1993.

The Daily Word

God gave the Apostle John a revelation to testify about Jesus Christ. The book of Revelation shares the vision the Lord entrusted to John. All who read, hear, and keep the words in the book of Revelation will be blessed because the time is near.

You may think the book of Revelation doesn't apply to you. Or you may assume it's over your head. You may even feel a sense of fear when you begin to think about the book of Revelation. However, John encouraged his readers by saying those who heed Revelation's words will be blessed because the time is near. John followed this by powerfully describing Jesus. Today, as you read John's descriptions of Christ, ask the Lord to expand your heart to this revelation entrusted to John—*Jesus is the One who is, who was, and who is coming. Jesus Christ is the faithful witness, the firstborn from the dead and the rulers of the kings of the earth. Jesus loves you and set you free from sins. He made you a kingdom and a priest to His God and Father. Jesus is coming on the clouds. Jesus is the Alpha and the Omega, the Almighty. Jesus is the Living One, alive forever, and He holds the keys of death and Hades.* Praise the mighty name of Jesus! Fall before the Lord as you enter into His presence in worship.

The one who reads this is blessed, and those who hear the words of this prophecy and keep what is written in it are blessed, because the time is near! —Revelation 1:3

Further Scripture: Matthew 5:6; Revelation 1:4–6, 17–18

Questions

1. This book is the Revelation of Jesus Christ (Revelation 1:1). What do you think we should be looking for to be revealed on every page? Note that in Revelation 1:19, John was instructed to write about what he had seen, what was, and what will happen.

2. In Revelation 1:3b; Scripture says, "the time is near." How much closer is this time now if it was "near" then? Do you agree that time is growing short before the return of the Lord? How does it make you feel to think Jesus could come back tomorrow? Are you ready? Why or why not?

3. How do you think Revelation 1:7 will happen? Do you think it will be possible for "every eye" to see or does it mean just those close by? Why do you think that?

4. What is the significance of a sharp two-edged sword in Revelation 1:16? Where else in Scripture is this sword referenced (Ephesians 6:17; Hebrews 4:12)?

5. At what point did Jesus get the keys to Hades/Hell as He says in Revelation 1:18 (Ephesians 4:8–9; 1 Peter 3:19–20; Revelation 20:1–2)?

6. What did the Holy Spirit highlight to you in Revelation 1 through the reading or the teaching?

Lesson 2: Revelation 2

I AM: The First Four Church Letters

Teaching Notes

Intro

The truth about studying Revelation is that no matter how long you study the book, you can always go back and learn more. In chapter 2, there are four churches in Asia to cover. In Revelation 1:19, John was instructed to "write what you have seen, things which are and are to come." The things that ARE were for the church-age and the dispensation of grace (Ephesians 3:2). That included the churches of the first century and the churches today. The book of Revelation draws God's master plan together. God is on the threshold of coming back. From the island of Patmos, John addressed each of the churches of Asia in a way that presented the information to each church in the order each might be visited. John typically used a pattern when writing to each church: (1) the commission to the church; (2) the character of Christ; (3) the commendation of the good things the church had done; (4) the condemnation of the bad things the church had done; (5) the correction of what the church should do; (6) the call to the church to hear what the Holy Spirit was saying, and (7) the challenge the church was to fulfill.

The role of the theologian is to study Scripture and interpret what it means. After having studied through 65 books of the Bible, you have the right to ask what God means in these passages as well.

Teaching

Revelation 2:1–7: There is much about the details of Revelation that are unknown. Verse 1 addressed the church in Ephesus, pointing out that Jesus held the seven stars in His right hand and walked among the seven golden candlesticks (seven churches). John knew the works of the church in Ephesus (v. 2). He knew what they engaged in and were willing to do for Christ's sake. I believe that every one of these churches, which are all different from each other, were considered to be good churches. The church had endured persecution and yet continued on (v. 3).

Nevertheless, the church in Ephesus had turned away from its first love (v. 4). It was an awesome church, but it had turned from Christ as its priority.

John chided them for having fallen away from Christ and instructed them to repent and return to doing "first works" for Him (v. 5). In this case, "repent" meant to turn away from the things that were against Christ and instead turn back to Christ. If the church didn't repent, Christ would remove their candlestick from the church. That action would kill the church. God does not threaten things that He is unwilling to do.

In verse 6, a reference is made to the Nicolaitans. It is possible they were a heretical sect and practiced sexual immorality, taught false doctrine, and ate meat that had been sacrificed to idols. The church was holding to doctrine but losing passion for the lost. Those that overcome the persecution for Christ were promised eternal life ("to eat of the tree of life") (v. 7).

Revelation 2:8–11: In verse 8, John wrote to the church in Smyrna. Christ knew the church's works and tribulations. And He knew about the blasphemy of those who claimed to be Jews but were instead of Satan (v. 9). Apparently, strong opposition from the Jewish sect in Smyrna had brought much hardship to the church. John warned that the Christians would suffer, but they should not be afraid. They would be cast into prison, tried, and, ten days later, would be executed. However, they were to be faithful even unto death, and then they would receive the crown of life (v. 10).

Revelation 2:12–17: In verse 12, John writes to the church in Pergamum and explained that Jesus' message was a sharp double-edged sword. Jesus knew the church's work and that the people lived in the area where Satan's throne was (possibly the center of the Babylonian cult) (v. 13). John commended the church for their work, and then moved to condemnation. The reference to Balaam and Balak is about the strength within the church. The church cannot be attacked in its strengths, but it can be attacked in its weaknesses (v. 14a). For the early church, those weaknesses were sexual sins, self-indulgence, and meat sacrificed to idols (v. 14b).

In reality, these things are still here for our churches to confront today. What are the strengths of your church and what are the weaknesses? The situation today has not changed from what the first-century churches faced.

The church in Pergamum had not dealt with the Nicolaitans like the Ephesians had, but had allowed their doctrines in the church (v. 15). John called them to repent immediately (v. 16). We don't know what the phrase "white stone" means, and we don't need to dwell on it. There are things of prophecy we cannot know.

Revelation 2:18–29: In verse 18, John writes to the church in Thyatira. John followed his pattern, acknowledging their good works, charity, service, faith, and patience (v. 19). They had even gotten better over time. He then gave condemnations. The people were being seduced into sexual sins and eating meat that had been sacrificed to idols, without regret or repentance (vv. 20–21). John explained that without repentance, they would face tribulation and death so that all the churches would know that Jesus is *I AM* and is in charge of them (v. 23). John then offered some hope—those who were not guilty of these sins would not face the same tribulations (v. 24). Those who kept God's commands would be blessed with authority over the nations and would be given the "morning star" (v. 28).

Closing

I pray that you would continue to look at this chapter to see what God has to say to you.

The Daily Word

John followed God's instructions to write and deliver letters to seven churches. As the Lord addressed the churches of Ephesus, Smyrna, Pergamum, and Thyatira, He repeated Himself with the phrase, "I know your . . ." Yes, the Lord knew their strengths, their works, how they stood strong in the place of suffering or temptation, and how they gave in. *Each church received a different challenge from the Lord.* Some He asked to repent. Others were encouraged to hold strong and be faithful until death because they would be victorious and would be granted a crown of life. John reminded the churches: "Anyone who has an ear should listen to what the Spirit says."

If you have received a convicting message from the Lord, perhaps through a friend, a sermon, or a post you read online, don't be ignorant and turn the other way. *Listen to the Holy Spirit's prompting.* You may be like the churches of Ephesus, Pergamum, or Thyatira, needing to repent and turn back to your first love, Jesus. Remember, God knows you. God knows your works, love, faithfulness, and endurance. He knows your affliction and poverty. He knows the temptations you face, and He knows all you tolerate. If God wrote *you* a letter, what would He say to you? How would you respond?

Anyone who has an ear should listen to what the Spirit says to the churches. —Revelation 2:29

Further Scripture: Psalm 26:2; Acts 3:19; Revelation 2:4

Questions

1. What did Jesus warn the church in Ephesus about? What had happened to them (Revelation 2:4–5)? What did He tell them to do?

2. What was happening to the church in Smyrna, and how did Jesus comfort them? Do you ever feel persecuted for your faith? How does it compare to the persecution that the church in Smyrna was experiencing or even how Christians in some parts of the world suffer today (Revelation 2:9–10)?

3. The church in Pergamum was faithful not to deny Jesus' name, even through the martyrdom of one of their people. What were they doing wrong that many churches do today (Revelation 2:14–15)?

4. Name some things the church of Thyatira was doing right (Revelation 2:19)? Despite these things, what was their downfall (Revelation 2:20–21)?

5. Look back at what John said would happen to the churches if they didn't turn from their wrongdoings. Could you possibly be attending one of these churches that fail to love God and people as they should, who compromise truth or are corrupt in their teachings?

6. What did the Holy Spirit highlight to you in Revelation 2 through the reading or the teaching?

Lesson 3: Revelation 3

I AM: Letters to Three More Churches

Teaching Notes

Intro

Today we continue by looking at the next three churches. In review, we've looked at the churches of: Ephesus—the loveless church; Smyrna—the stalwart church; Pergamum—the compromising church; and Thyatira—the moral compromise church. John used a uniform outline that was developed by Tenney: (1) commission; (2) character; (3) commendation; (4) condemnation; (5) correction; (6) call; and (7) challenge.[1] Today, the call and the challenge are inverted.

Teaching

Revelation 3:1–6: John next addressed the church in Sardis. In verse 1 Jesus described Himself to John as, "the One who has the seven spirits of God and the seven stars." The book of 1 Enoch 20:1–8, one of the Hebrew texts found in the Dead Sea Scrolls, names the seven angels: Uriel, Raphael, Raguel, Michael, Saraqael, Gabriel, and Remiel. In Revelation 8:2, these are the angels who blow the trumpets. Throughout Revelation the number seven is used. So far, we've seen seven spirits/seven stars; sevenfold operation of the Spirit (Isaiah 11:2); and seven archangels of Jewish tradition. There are more sevens to come in Revelation 4—5.

Jesus commended Sardis for their works and their reputation of being alive. Everything provided about each church gives information about its city and its context. You may note some similarities between the churches of Ephesus and Sardis. Sardis was located 50 miles northeast of Ephesus, and its geographic backdrop contained three main landmarks: (1) an acropolis that rose 800 feet above the city and had nearly perpendicular rock walls on three sides, creating a natural citadel; (2) the temple to Artemis, which was unfinished and built over the top of an older temple to Cybele (a god who was believed to possess special power of restoring dead to life); and (3) the Necropolis or cemetery of 1,000 hills—burial mounds that could be seen on the skyline seven miles from the city. John then

---

[1] Merrill C. Tenney, *Interpreting Revelation* (Grand Rapids, MI: Wm. B. Eerdmans, 1951), n.p.

gave the condemnation that although the church was believed to be alive, it was dead. The church had retained an outward appearance of life while being dead inside. Some regard this as the most severe condemnation of the seven churches (v. 3). Sardis was a city of pride, arrogance, and wealth that relied heavily on their past accomplishments and past reputation. The danger was that the church now reflected the city more than it reflected Christ.

Note that of the seven churches, five needed renewal, and that was only after 60 years into the history of the Church. The problem of church renewal is nothing new. Christ's heart broke when thinking of this congregation—who was a bride in name only. Jesus told them to wake up to the urgent need because they were under attack. They needed to stay alert (v. 3). Jesus reminded them of attacks against the city that they had already faced. One story told of how Cyrus captured the city by sending a climber up a crevice on one of the most perpendicular walls—most formidable to climb—of the fortress. Later the same thing happened with the Romans. The warning is that to consider oneself secure and then fail to remain alert was to court disaster. In AD 17, Sardis experienced a catastrophic earthquake. The city was later rebuilt with considerable help from Emperor Tiberius, but it never fully recovered. In fact, the city remained incomplete and was never totally rebuilt. If the church did not become alert, Jesus would come at an unforeseen moment to judge them.

The church today struggles with apathy. What appearances do we have, to keep up? Is there a sneak attack coming where we don't even look? Are we dead on the inside? The church of Sardis had a few people (the remnant) who walked faithfully and would walk in white with Christ because they are worthy (v. 4). In Asia Minor, soiled clothes disqualified the worshipper and dishonored the gods. White garments were emblems of purity and victory (Revelation 19:8). White clothes are mentioned seven times in Revelation: 3:4–5; 4:4; 6:11; 7:9, 13; and 19:14. The challenge was to remain faithful and be victorious. They would have their name added to the Book of Life for their faithfulness (v. 5). His message is vital for all of us to hear. Note: The first reference to the Book of Life is in Exodus 32:32–33.

Revelation 3:7–13: John then addressed the church in Philadelphia, which was located at the eastern end of the same valley as the town of Sardis. Philadelphia was located at a junction of trade routes—the imperial post route from Rome passed through the city, earning the city the title "Gateway to the East." The city had commercial importance. To the north of the city was a fertile plain on which grapes were grown. It was founded by the king of Pergamum to commemorate the sacrificial loyalty and devotion of his brother. However, the area was subject to earthquakes and also suffered terribly from the AD 17 earthquake. It also had so many temples that by the fifth century it was known as "Little Athens."

The chief god worshipped, because of the grapes grown there, was Dionysus, the god of wine and fertility?

Once again, Jesus, the *I AM*, addressed the church. This description includes Jesus as the One who holds the key of David. The word for key included the key and the doorknob as well (v. 7). That alludes to the fact that the Messiah controls access to the eternal kingdom. Jesus has undisputed authority to admit or exclude anyone from the New Jerusalem. This is also a direct reference to Isaiah 22:15–22, in which a promise was made to Eliakim the scribe of the court of Hezekiah. Jesus acknowledged their faithfulness by giving them access to the open door. In spite of feeble strength, the church had refused to deny the name of Christ and would not allow it to be removed (v. 8). Remember, in the event of an earthquake, the safest place to be is in the doorframe.

The Lord would make those who came from Satan bow before the feet of the Christians. Verses 9–10 point to the serious conflict between the church and the "synagogue of Satan." However, the believers had persevered in times of trial. Dispensationalists have used this passage as proof for a rapture before the tribulation, but the Greek doesn't lend to that interpretation. That doesn't disprove their thoughts, but it cannot be proved by verse 10. Jesus promised that He was coming quickly and that His strength would be added to their weakness. It is interesting to note that a Christian witness remained in Pergamum through medieval and into modern times—despite the Muslim invasion and their pressure on the church. Jesus promised to make them the victors with the crown of life. Notice there was no condemnation or correction given. For the victor, there was a threefold inscription given: the name of His God because of their faithfulness; the name of God's city because of their citizenship in New Jerusalem; and His own new name because they were related in a special way to Christ (Revelation 7:3; 14:1). The church at Philadelphia was the faithful, courageous, and humble church. Jesus therefore promised to use them in powerful ways. The key to effectiveness for any church is to realize how powerless we are without the power of the Holy Spirit, who exhibits His strength through us.

Revelation 3:14–22: John's seventh and final letter was to the church in Laodicea. This church was in the wealthy Roman city that had acquired earthly power by wealth. Jesus was again described as the *I AM*—the amen. Jesus knew their works and said they were neither cold nor hot. Their faithfulness was lukewarm at best. Jesus said He would vomit them from His mouth. The word vomit here means to spit out with force. Their wealth became a limiting factor of what they were willing to do (v. 17). Lukewarm is best interpreted against the local geography. To the north were healthy hot springs at Hierapolis, and to the south were cold springs that were clean and refreshing to drink from. Laodicea had perpetual problems with its water supply, which came by aqueduct six miles from the south. The water was lukewarm, unclean, undrinkable, and could make a person sick. They were so prosperous and powerful that they assumed they had spiritual success. They were ignorant of God's view of their prosperity. They were spiritually poor, blind, and naked because of being blinded by their wealth.

Closing

The condemnation and the call are God's love languages to bring us back into relationship with Him. Repent! Jesus stands at the door and knocks. Anyone who hears His voice and opens the door to Him will be saved. We are called to be overcomers and victors and are promised eternal life with Him!

The Daily Word

The letters continue to unfold as John proclaimed his vision from the Lord to the three remaining churches: Sardis, Philadelphia, and Laodicea. Each had a different challenge: to be alert and strengthen what remained; to endure all things by keeping God's command with faithful, courageous, and humble love; and to repent from a lukewarm way of life and be committed to Jesus.

Specifically, the Lord declared to the church of Laodicea, "Listen! I stand at the door and knock. If anyone hears My voice and opens the door, I will come in to him and have dinner with him, and he with Me." *This message is for you.* Do you know the voice of the Shepherd? Jesus said, "My sheep hear My voice, I know them, and they follow Me." Today, do you hear the voice of the Lord? Do you hear the Lord knocking? Take time to pause from the busyness and sit quietly. Ask the Lord: *Jesus, what do You want me to know about You? If we were having dinner, what would You say to me?* When you ask these questions, sit and listen like you would to a friend. Today, listen to the One who guides you, knows you, and loves you. Remain alert and ready.

As many as I love, I rebuke and discipline. So be committed and repent. Listen! I stand at the door and knock. If anyone hears My voice and opens the door, I will come in to him and have dinner with him, and he with Me. —Revelation 3:19–20

Further Scripture: John 10:3–4; Revelation 3:2–3, 15–16

Questions

1. Even though the church in Sardis seemed active and alive, inside they were spiritually dead. Do you know any churches like this today? What did John say will happen to them (Revelation 3:3)?

2. Why was the Lord pleased with the church of Philadelphia? What did He promise them (Revelation 3:10)?

3. What did the Lord say about the lukewarm church (Revelation 3:15–17)? What is the spiritual temperature of your church?

4. What does Jesus promise to those who overcome and endure to the end (Revelation 2:7, 11, 17, 26; 3:5, 12, 21)?

5. Which message, to these churches, speaks most directly to you about your church and the condition of your own spiritual position? What will you do to change this?

6. What did the Holy Spirit highlight to you in Revelation 3 through the reading or the teaching?

Lesson 4: Revelation 4

I AM: The Throne Room of Heaven

Teaching Notes

Intro

The Garden in Genesis ties into Revelation as it pointed to the Messiah. In Revelation 4, John had a vision of Christ. Christ told John to talk to His seven churches. The seven churches were similar to the Israelites who kept turning away from God. The churches believed in Christ but, at some point, they turned away from Him.

Revelation 1:19 outlines the entire book, and chapter 4 gives the third part of what would take place for each of the seven churches. Revelation 1:19 basically asked the question: "What will take place next?" These verses are about what is to come—a future word that would come to fruition.

Teaching

Revelation 4:1–11: Revelation 4 contains a vision of what worshipping in heaven will be like. John saw an open door because Christ would no longer be knocking. The open door was a vision of welcoming the redeemed into the presence of God. God's voice sounded like a trumpet. According to Warren Wiersbe, the invitation is a picture of God on His throne.[1]

In verse 2 John was now in the spirit. According to John MacArthur, John allowed all of his senses to be taken over by God: "This was not a dream. John was supernaturally transported out of the material world awake—not sleeping—to an experience beyond the normal senses. The Holy Spirit empowered his senses to perceive revelation from God (cf. Acts 10:11)."[2] All of John's senses were heightened. There would be some practical function for every prophetic word. This took place in the third heaven where God was seated on His throne.

---

[1] Warren W. Wiersbe, *The Bible Exposition Commentary: Ephesians–Revelation* (Colorado Springs: David C. Cook, 2003), 528.

[2] John MacArthur, *The MacArthur Bible Commentary* (Nashville: Thomas Nelson, 2005), 2002.

Verse 3 describes what surrounded the throne. The one seated there was like precious stones, jasper, and carnelian. Jasper is described as being crystal clear, similar to a diamond. MacArthur states, "John describes this stone as 'crystal clear' (21:11), probably referring to a diamond, which refracts all the colors of the spectrum in wondrous brilliance."[3] The carnelian stone has a fiery, ruby color, so it appeared as fire.

MacArthur also explains that "a cool, emerald-green hue dominates the multicolored rainbow surrounding God's throne (cf. Ezekiel 1:28). From the time of Noah, the rainbow became a sign of God's faithfulness to His Word, His promises, and His Noahic covenant (Genesis 9:12–17)."[4] As humans, it is difficult to understand the image of God on His throne.

While he was stranded on an island, because he was preaching the gospel too much, John received the vision from an angel. God was on His throne, He looked like a clear diamond stone, and He was surrounded by an emerald green rainbow. The true image of what John saw was indescribable.

Around the throne of God were an additional 24 thrones. Elders, in white robes and with golden crowns, sat on each of the thrones. These may have represented some kind of purity or righteousness. They also may have represented the redeemed. MacArthur points out, "The question is which redeemed? Not Israel, since the nation is not yet saved, glorified, and coronated."[5]

Nelson's Commentary explains, "The identity of the elders is not certain. Some think that they represent the church or believers in heaven, but it seems preferable to view the elders as angels who comprise a heavenly ruling council (Jeremiah 23:18, 22)."[6] Scholars have different perspectives. Regardless of their interpretations, they agree that God has chosen these 24 elders to surround the throne.

In verse 5, flashes of lightening appear. Then seven spirits of God appear. *Nelson's Commentary* explains, "Seven Spirits of God as represented by seven lamps presents the fullness of the sevenfold character of the Holy Spirit (Isaiah 11:2, 3)."[7] No one knows for sure what the seven spirits represent.

In verse 6, a sea of glass, like crystal, was before the throne. Revelation 21:1 explains that the sea would no longer exist. Therefore, the image of the crystal before the throne was not water.

Four creatures full of eyes and who are able to see everything will appear. The creatures each had six wings. According to *Nelson's Commentary*, "The lion, calf,

---

[3] MacArthur, 2002.

[4] MacArthur, 2002.

[5] MacArthur, 2002.

[6] Earl Radmacher, Ronald B. Allen, and H. Wayne House, eds., *Nelson's New Illustrated Bible Commentary* (Nashville: Thomas Nelson, 1999), 1742.

[7] Radmacher et al., 1742.

man, and eagle have been understood as referring to the four Gospels with their distinctive portrayals of Christ."[8] The creatures sing hymns.

Verse 10 states the elders will cast their crowns before the throne. They were aware that everything came from God. Then the elders started to sing with the four creatures.

Closing

The singing was worship before the Lord and God got all the glory. This worship happens day and night and never stops. John saw these images and with no one to tell he wrote it all down. All who were present experienced the presence of the living God. God alone was worthy to receive the glory, honor, and power.

Revelation 1 is where John received the vision from Christ. Revelation 2—3 is about the churches keeping their eyes on Christ. Revelation 4 describes John's view of the throne, those who were present and what was taking place.

The Daily Word

Imagine John all alone on an island when the Spirit of God entrusted him with visions of what was to come and instructions to send his visions to the seven churches of Asia. As John was in the Spirit, he saw the One seated on a throne encircled by 24 elders on 24 thrones. He described four living creatures continuously saying, "Holy, holy, holy, Lord God Almighty, who was, and is, and who is coming." The 24 elders cast their earned crowns before the throne of the One and proclaim, "Our Lord and God, You are worthy to receive glory and honor and power, because You have created all things."

You may not physically be gathered around the throne of heaven, but you can take time to worship the Lord. Posture yourself to worship Him. Give Him the "crowns" in your life. Whatever you feel you have gained, *surrender it all to the Lord.* Give thanks to the Lord. Recognize God as the author and creator of all things, who is deserving of all honor, power, and glory. Worship Him because He is truly worthy of it all. This life is not about you on earth, it is about the Lord and His kingdom that is to come in heaven. Day and night, let your praise rise to the one who is worthy of it all.

The 24 elders fall down before the One seated on the throne, worship the One who lives forever and ever, cast their crowns before the throne, and say:
> **Our Lord and God,**
> **You are worthy to receive**
> **glory and honor and power,**

---

[8] Radmacher et al., 1742.

because You have created all things,
and because of Your will
they exist and were created. —Revelation 4:10–11

Further Scripture: Jeremiah 10:7; Colossians 1:16; Revelation 4:8

Questions

1. John was shown a throne in heaven with a rainbow around it. What connection, if any, do you think this rainbow has with the covenant God made with Noah and all humankind (Genesis 9:11–17)? Look into what the significance is of the rainbow's color (emerald) and the stones used to describe the One sitting on the throne in Revelation 4:3. (**Note:** The rainbow around the throne is shades of green. Green represents grace/mercy. The colors emanating from the One who sits on the throne are carnelian [a deep red] signifying God's wrath [justice], which man does not want to approach, and jasper [diamond, clear, and white light] signifying God's purity and righteousness, which man cannot approach. Yet in Hebrews we are told we can confidently approach the throne of grace [Hebrews 4:16]. So, the emerald rainbow of God's grace is a picture of what makes that possible.)

2. Do you think the 24 elders were representatives of a group of people or were specific people? What do you think their crowns signified (2 Timothy 4:8)?

3. Where else in Scripture do we see a description similar to Revelation 4:5a (Exodus 19:16; Hebrews 12:18–19)?

4. There was a sea of glass like crystal before the throne. Do you think the bronze laver, also known as the bronze sea, was a shadow or symbol of this sea of glass? What was the purpose of the bronze laver or sea (Exodus 30:18–21; 2 Kings 25:13; Hebrews 8:5)?

5. As the four living creatures give glory and honor and thanks to Him who sits on the throne, what will the 24 elders be doing (Revelation 4:9–11)? Why do you think John was shown this?

6. What did the Holy Spirit highlight to you in Revelation 4 through the reading or the teaching?

Lesson 5: Revelation 5

I AM: Worship in Heaven

Teaching Notes

Intro

Most of the message in Revelation is about what has yet to come. Throughout history, we have the accounts of Moses when he went up on the mountain and God gave him the account of what was before his time, from the ancient past and in the beginning. That is found in Genesis.

In the New Testament, the Apostle Paul gave account of the distant past and the message to the church. Paul gave instruction on the formation of the church and he included the disciplines of the church age. Now, in Revelation, the Apostle John was given the account of what was to come. From these three writers of Scripture came the explanations of who God was, who God is, and who God is yet to come.

In the first four chapters of Revelation, John explained who Jesus is and what He looks like. Christ is the Word of God. Chapter 4 gives the description and explanation of the image of God on His throne.

Teaching

Revelation 5:1–14: Chapter 5 is to be the action plan that followed after the explanation of Christ's appearance. John came into a throne room scene, and then the scene went into action with the four beasts and the 24 elders. John joined the audience before the throne.

John saw God on the throne, and in His right hand was a book. This book would have been a scroll written on both sides and sealed with seven seals. In verse 2 an angel cried out, "Who is worthy to open the book and loosen the seals?" There is required criteria for an individual to open the seals. The comparison would be similar to someone who had the authority to open up a scroll that was sealed with the king's signet.

The desire of all was to know what was in the scroll, but no one had the authority or was worthy to open the scroll. All the observers except the elders were weeping. The answer came from one of the elders–Christ was present and was able and worthy to open the scroll. Verse 6 describes the Lamb of God, as though He had been slain, and with seven horns and seven eyes, at the throne in the midst of the audience of elders and beasts. The appearance of the marks from the crucifixion may have given the impression of having been slain. The seven horns and eyes represented the seven spirits of God. Isaiah 11 includes a list of the seven spirits.

The seven spirits of God could be contrasted to the evil spirits found in Numbers 5; Isaiah 4, 29, and 61; Hosea 5; Luke 13; Acts 16; Romans 11; 2 Timothy 1; and 1 John. The seven spirits of God include: the Spirit of the Lord, wisdom, understanding, counsel, might, knowledge, and fear of God. The spirits of evil include: jealousy, judgment, burning, heaviness, whoredom, infirmity, divination, slumber, fear, and the Antichrist.

God sends His influence in spirit all over the earth, especially to those in the church because they're already born of the Spirit of God, and the Spirit of God would have a home or dwelling place in them. The influence of the Spirit would automatically be in them. When prayer walking, you can ask God to fill those areas with His seven spirits.

Matthew 12:44 outlines the casting out of evil spirits. There is a strategy in the spirits for having authority. A reasonable application would include comparing the list of the spirits of God against the life of the believer. The question would be, what is the evidence of the spirits of God in the life of believers and leaders? The importance of the seven spirits is to offer believers evidence of the working of God in their lives.

The Lamb in Revelation represents Christ. The 24 elders in Revelation could represent the 12 tribes of Israel and the 12 apostles. The 24 become the witnesses. The price Christ paid through the crucifixion gives Him the authority to open the scroll and break the seals.

In verse 8, Christ took the scroll, and the 24 elders and the four beasts bowed down before the Lamb. They had harps, and they sang a new song proclaiming Christ's authority. They had bowls of incense and offered them up to Christ. Christ's victory made the believers a kingdom and priests before God.

The text in verse 11 states that a choir of more than a 100 million sang, "Worthy is the Lamb." Seven attributes are mentioned in the song. The list of attributes included: power, riches, wisdom, strength, honor, glory, and blessing.

There was something that was coming together. The One on the throne no longer held the scroll. The Lamb in front now held the scroll, while the four beasts praised God and the 24 elders worshipped the Lamb.

Closing

Those who have suffered for their faith will hear the songs of praise, and they will rejoice. All those present will worship at the throne of God. Chapter 5 gives an image of the worship of God that begins at this point. Next, the stage is set for deeper things that are to come.

The Daily Word

As John's vision continued, one of the elders declared who was worthy to open the scroll and break its seal: "The Lion from the tribe of Judah, the Root of David, has been victorious so that He may open the scroll and its seven seals." Jesus, the Lamb, is worthy to open the scroll. He was slaughtered, and His blood redeems people from every tribe and language and nation for God. Yes, indeed, Jesus alone is worthy. John witnessed an angelic choir worshipping: "The Lamb who was slaughtered is worthy to receive power and riches and wisdom and strength and honor and glory and blessing!"

You may face suffering, trials, persecution, and unmet expectations. For a moment, rest in the hope of heaven. *There will be a day when the whole earth will worship the One who is worthy, the Lamb of God.* Picture this moment of worship in heaven. Reflect on His redemption in your life. Jesus is worthy to receive power, riches, wisdom, strength, honor, glory, and blessing. Will you stand to worship, or will you fall down to worship Him? Give Jesus your whole heart as you worship Him today. He is worthy of it all.

Then one of the elders said to me, "Stop crying. Look! The Lion from the tribe of Judah, the Root of David, has been victorious so that He may open the scroll and its seven seals." —Revelation 5:5

Further Scripture: Genesis 49:9–10; John 1:29; Revelation 5:11–12

Questions

1. It first appeared that the book in the hand of Him who sits on the throne could not be opened. Why couldn't it be opened, according to Revelation 5:4?

2. Who is the One who has overcome so as to open the book and its seals (Revelation 5:5)?

3. What was the response of the 24 elders and the four living creatures to the Lamb (Revelation 5:8)?

4. What did the Lamb purchase for God, and what did He pay with (Revelation 5:9)?

5. Compare what is being said to the Lamb in Revelation 5:12 with what is being said to God in Revelation 4:11. What do you think the significance of the word "worthy" is in both these sayings?

6. In Revelation 5:13, every created thing that was in heaven, on earth or under the earth, and on the sea and all things in them are saying what and to whom? What do you think "every created thing" means?

7. What did the Holy Spirit highlight to you in Revelation 5 through the reading or the teaching?

Lesson 6: Revelation 6

I AM: The Word for Revelation: I AM

Teaching Notes

Intro

A transition started in chapters 4 and 5. Chapter 6 is not the first chapter of a new book, but it is the chapter of a new section and a change. The first three chapters of Revelation presented the image of Christ and His concern for the churches. Chapter 4 and 5 included the unique imagery of the throne with all the sights and sounds.

Chapter 6 begins the apocalyptic writing of John. Smith and Card note the difficulty of studying this section of Revelation:

> You read chapters 4 and 5, and even though much of the imagery seems rather strange, there is still a sense that Revelation is not such a formidable and unfriendly part of the Bible. In fact, your heart is actually encouraged and stirred as you ponder the inviting sights and sounds of the throne room vision. . . . But then you resume your reading at chapter 6 and before long, you hit the "Revelation wall." Lost in the mire of "seals," "trumpets," and "woes" you are tempted to run to the safe and predictable harbors of the Gospel of John or the Psalms.[1]

Chapter 6 includes poetry, imagery, and a different type of literature than most individuals would be familiar with. Nothing in apocalyptic literature comes from a normal pattern.

The flow of writing in chapter 6 can be seen from multiple points of view. There is a possibility of a chronological timeline. Another option would be to interpret the "seals," "trumpets," and "bowls," as all referring to the same thing, similar to how the four Gospels tell the same story but in four different ways. A third option would be to see chapter 6 as a spiral writing style.

Lizorkin-Eyzenberg notes that

---

[1] Scotty Smith and Michael Card, *Unveiled Hope* (Nashville: Thomas Nelson, 1997), 106.

the readers should know that near eastern and Jewish conceptions of time are cyclical rather than linear. The fulfillments of prophecies or promises could occur once and then reoccur multiple times throughout history in various ways until "the end of the age." This is not helpful in creation of timelines and the book should not be read with the linear and sequential view of time in mind. . . . Much like the Hebrew prophets, John addresses people and issues of his own day (the present) while also incorporating Israel's history of covenantal relationship with God (the past) and the predicted final judgment, restoration, and covenantal fulfillment (the future). Remember in Jewish thought, history is not linear nor circular, but spiral like. A prophesy can speak about past, present, and future simultaneously.[2]

Revelation addressed first-century Christians directly. It presented timeless truths for surviving the struggle between good and evil. It also had much to say about what was yet to come. The way one looked at Revelation had an impact on how it was received. It is best to read chapters 6—11 in one sitting to understand the flow.

Teaching

Revelation 6:1–17: The visions of the seals was coming from the throne room. The scroll was sealed with seven seals. The first seal was opened by the Lamb. As the seal was opened, one of the creatures called out like thunder, "Come." The opening of the first seal brought forth a horseman with a bow, riding on a white horse. This was the first of the four horsemen of the apocalypse.

The imagery of the horses in verses 1–8, is similar to the imagery found in Zechariah 1:8–17. Zechariah saw images of variously colored horses of red, sorrel, white, dappled gray, and black. In Revelation, the color of the horses coincides with the character of the rider—conquest was white, bloodshed was red, scarcity was black, and death was pale green (v. 8).

Mounce explains that in Zechariah, the horsemen were to patrol the earth, while in Revelation, the horsemen were to release the disasters upon the earth.[3] The form of John's vision was related to Zechariah, but the subject matter of Revelation was Jesus' teaching from the Gospels about the end times.

---

[2] Eli Lizorkin-Eyzenberg, "Revelation in Its Jewish Context I," see under "Materials: Lecture Notes for This Course," Israel Bible Center, 53, 114, https://d1u2upkuheb556.cloudfront.net/All+Course+PDF+Notes/Revelation1.pdf.

[3] Robert H. Mounce, *The Book of Revelation*, The New International Commentary on the New Testament (Grand Rapids, MI: Wm. B. Eerdmans, 1997), 152.

The horseman comes out with a crown and a bow. This has relevance to Revelation 19. The one who said *I AM* was riding a white horse. The rider in chapter 6 also rode a white horse, and he represented the Antichrist. This rider on a white horse brought about destruction.

There may be a connection between the Four Horsemen of the Apocalypse and the seventieth week of Daniel. The horseman on the white horse would have been the final satanic dictator over men.

The second seal was opened, a creature shouted, "Come," and a horseman on a red horse appears. His role was to take peace from the people. The color represented bloodshed and slaughter. This fiery red horse represented war. In 2 Thessalonians 2:6–12, Paul warned of the removal of peace. The people of the first century would have been familiar with this context.

The third seal was opened. A creature shouted, "Come," and a horseman on a black horse came forth. The black horse represented scarcity, inequity, and famine. The horseman had a balance scale. The description was similar to the passages in Ezekiel 4:6–11, when bread was eaten by weight and a drink of water was measured.

Mounce explains that the reference from Cicero was that prices were ten to 12 times what they should have been.[4] The olive oil and the wine were basic commodities and not luxuries. They were to be used sparingly.

The fourth seal was opened, and the fourth creature shouted, "Come." A horseman on a pale green horse appeared who represented Death and Hades. He had authority to kill by the sword, famine, plagues, and wild animals. This horseman was given authority over a fourth of the earth. This completes the information on the four horsemen in Scripture.

The fifth seal was opened. An altar in heaven appeared, and under it were the faithful martyrs. They were given white robes and told to wait a little while longer. The white robes symbolized their purity and blessedness.

The seven seals were divided into two groups, the first four and last three. The four horsemen were the first four seals. Various scenes are portrayed at the opening of each of the three remaining seals.

Seal six was opened, and an earthquake occurred. The sun turned black, and the moon became like blood. A breakdown of all created order began to occur, announcing that the end of world was at hand. The people feared facing the wrath of the Lord. They longed for death by any means other than facing God's wrath.

_____

[4] Mounce, 155.

Closing

Only the believer can stand against the great judgment of the Lord. This requires justification by grace and through faith in Jesus Christ.

God is in control no matter how things look. Those that have been declared righteous by faith have peace with God through our Lord Jesus Christ.

The Daily Word

Just as it was determined, the Lamb opened the six seals of the scroll. Each seal revealed something to come: conquest and overturn of power, war, famine, scarcity, death, martyrdom, and wrath. Not one of the seals reveled something enjoyable or comfortable. Each one would bring fear and pain. *You may wonder who is able to stand under all the hardship.* Who is able to withstand the pain of what is to come?

You are able to stand up and endure because of your faith in Jesus Christ. Paul encouraged believers to stand strong in the Lord and in His strength during battle. The Lord equips your hands for battle. The Name of the Lord is a strong tower you can run to and hide in. He will protect you. The Lord is a stronghold in the day of distress because He cares for all who take refuge in Him. You are declared righteous by faith. Through your faith, you are justified and have peace with God through Jesus Christ. Rejoice in the hope of glory, no matter how bleak life may appear. Remember, God remains in control; you can stand in Him and in His promises. He is with you and will never leave you nor forsake you.

And they said to the mountains and to the rocks, "Fall on us and hide us from the face of the One seated on the throne and from the wrath of the Lamb, because the great day of Their wrath has come! And who is able to stand?" —Revelation 6:16–17

Further Scripture: Proverbs 18:10; Nahum 1:6–7; Ephesians 6:10

Questions

1. Jesus was found to be the only One worthy to open the scrolls. What were God's future judgments from each of the first six scrolls described in Revelation 6?

2. How was the voice of the creature in the first seal described? What adjectives were used to describe voices in heaven (Revelation 1:10; 4:1)?

3. How were the riders on the horses described in Revelation 6? How is each one unique?

4. What did the white robe represent in Revelation 6:11 (Revelation 3:4; 7:9, 13–14; 19:8, 14)?

5. What did those mentioned in Revelation 6:16 mistakenly cry out to? Why do you think they would not cry out to the Lord (Romans 1:18–25)?

6. What did the Holy Spirit highlight to you in Revelation 6 through the reading or the teaching?

Lesson 7: Revelation 7

I AM: A Multitude from the Great Tribulation

Teaching Notes

Intro

As I prepared for this week's lessons, I'm convinced that this is probably the most meat we've had to chew on so far in reviveSCHOOL.

I pulled together about 30 charts from different institutions and theologians on the end times. As I laid these out and started comparing them, I noticed that they don't follow what is presented in Revelation. Just a reminder to us all that if something doesn't make sense, pull back a little and take time to consider what you're reading and hearing. I think the reason no one's timeline matches up to Revelation is because no one knows God's timeline. I do believe that as we get closer to the end times, more and more will become clear. I think it's all just starting.

Our phrase for how Jesus is seen in Revelation is *I AM* (Revelation 1:7–8). In chapters 6 and beyond is the picture of how Jesus will reveal Himself. Christ said, "*I AM* the beginning and the end."

Tom Schiefer led us through the six of the seven seals. Chapter 7 provides a pause in the giving of the seals. Only Jesus is worthy to open up the seals. Each scroll is opened completely to reveal what's inside. The first six seals are:

1. The first horseman on a white horse appears and is the Antichrist. This parallels Matthew 24 to Revelation 6 and is the beginning of the seven-year period of tribulation. The Great Tribulation begins halfway through that seven-year period.

2. A second horseman on a red horse appears to take peace from the people—there will be wars and rumors of wars (Matthew 26).

3. A third horseman on a black horse with a balance scale represents scarcity, inequity, and famine (6:5–6).

4. A fourth horseman on a pale green horse appears who represents death and hades.

5. An altar in heaven appears with faithful martyrs under it (Matthew 24:9; Revelation 6:9–11). We can't be sure of the timeline of all this, but we can be sure that believers will feel the fury during the fifth and sixth seals.

6. An earthquake occurs, the sun turns black, the moon becomes like blood, and a breakdown of all created order begins, announcing the end of the world is at hand.

Teaching

Revelation 7:1–8: In Revelation 7 there are two main groups—the 144,000 Jewish evangelists and the great multitude who put their trust in Jesus. This happens before the seventh seal is opened and God's wrath is released. John saw four angels standing at the four corners of the earth who were restraining the four winds (Revelation 14:18). A fifth angel rose up from the east holding a seal who cried out to the four angels who had the power to harm earth and seas not to harm anything until the seal had been placed by God on the foreheads of the 144,000 from every tribe of the Israelites.

Scholars disagree about how to understand the 144,000. Some say it is literal 144,000 people, and others say it is a symbolic number. I would like it to be a literal 144,000, because that just feels right to me. In Genesis 12 and 49, God promised that He would spare His people. Why wouldn't it make sense that God will raise a remnant up from each of the 12 tribes?

Revelation 7:9–10: Verse 9 begins a shift. Even with all the things that will happen, there will always be a remnant that will survive. God will use a little group to bring the people to Him. The seals reflect the birthing pains of this new age to come. John then saw a vast multitude from every nation, tribe, people, and language—so vast no one could number—who were standing before the throne and before the Lamb. They were robed in white and held palm branches (v. 9). Currently there's almost 200 nations and thousands of languages on earth.

The multitude cried out in a loud voice that salvation belongs to God who is seated on the throne and to the Lamb (v. 10). More than likely, these are people who have come to know Christ, possibly even martyred.

Revelation 7:11–14: The angels stood around the throne with the elders and the four living creatures, and they fell on their faces and worshipped God (vv. 11–12). One of the elders asked who all these people robed in white were (v. 13). John responded to the elder, "Sir, you know." The elder responded that these had come out of the great tribulation. Their robes had been washed in the blood of the Lamb (v. 14).

Revelation 7:16–18: Because of their salvation, they are before the throne of God and serve Him day and night. And He will shelter them (v. 15). They will no longer be hungry or thirsty, and the sun will no longer strike them (v. 16). This is a description of what they had experienced in the tribulation. The Lamb will take care of them and will guide them to springs of living waters. God will wipe every tear from their eyes (v. 17).

Closing

So we've seen two groups of people here: the 144,000 Jewish evangelists from the 12 tribes and the vast multitude. Tomorrow, chapter 8 reveals the seventh seal.

The Daily Word

After the sixth seal was opened, John described an angel from the east sealing 144,000 servants of God from every tribe of Israel. Then he described *a vast multitude from every nation, tribe, people, and language standing before the throne* and before the Lamb in heaven. The Lamb refers to Jesus, the redemptive sacrifice for the whole earth. Robed in white, the innumerable crowd cried out in a loud voice, "Salvation belongs to our God, who is seated on the throne, and to the Lamb!"

How will a "vast multitude from every nation, tribe, people, and language" know about the Lamb? This image seems to fulfill Jesus' Great Commission to His disciples to *go* because all authority had been given to make disciples of all nations. Even today, Jesus commands believers to *go* and share God's love to the nations. Who in your life needs to hear about Jesus, the sacrificial Lamb of God, who died for the sins of every nation, tribe, people, and language, offering redemption and eternal life? As you *go* and share, you will receive power from the Holy Spirit to bear witness wherever the Lord leads you. Today, it's time to *go*.

After this I looked, and there was a vast multitude from every nation, tribe, people, and language, which no one could number, standing before the throne and before the Lamb. They were robed in white with palm branches in their hands. And they cried out in a loud voice: Salvation belongs to our God, who is seated on the throne, and to the Lamb! —Revelation 7:9–10

Further Scripture: Matthew 28:19–20; Acts 1:8; Revelation 7:3–4

Questions

1. What did the angel, with the seal of the living God, tell the four angels who had been given power to hurt the earth and sea (Revelation 7:2–3)?

2. Twelve thousand from each of the 12 tribes will be sealed on their foreheads. What do we know about these seals (Revelation 14:1)? Look at Ezekiel 9:4. How was this situation similar? According to John 6:27b; 2 Corinthians 1:21–22; and Ephesians 1:13, who else has been sealed?

3. Do you believe these 144,000 are actual Israelites or are symbolic of the church or other group? What specific descriptions are given about these in Revelation 7:3–8 and 14:1–5?

4. A multitude is described in Revelation 7:9–10. What details are given? In Revelation 7:14–17, what was John told about this multitude?

5. Even though these came out of great tribulation, according to Revelation 7:14, to what or to whom do they attribute their salvation (Revelation 7:10)?

6. What did the Holy Spirit highlight to you in Revelation 7 through the reading or the teaching?

Lesson 8: Revelation 8

I AM: The Trumpet Judgment Begins

Teaching Notes

Intro

Revelation can sometimes feel like drinking from a fire hydrant. It is difficult to take everything in! It's encouraging to remember the promise of Revelation 1:3: "The one who reads this is blessed, and those who hear the words of this prophecy and keep what is written in it are blessed, because the time is near." The promise of being blessed just by reading Revelation will be repeated seven times throughout the book.

Our phrase for the book of Revelation is *I AM*. If you understand that Jesus is the beginning and the end, you will be blessed. Don't avoid Revelation because you aren't sure of your position on the end times. To be ready for the return of Christ, we have to embrace the hard things. Our hope in this study of Revelation is to help demystify the intimidating words like premillennial and pre-tribulation.

Over the last few days we've studied about six seals that would be unleashed over a period of seven years. We see 1,260 days mentioned a lot in Revelation. This is significant because it is 3.5 years, or half of the entire seven-year period known as the Tribulation. At this point in John's vision, the Antichrist is on the earth. A lot has already been happening. There have been famines, war, and death. Crazy things have happened in nature. Once the first 1,260 days pass, the second half of the Tribulation is known as the Great Tribulation. In the Great Tribulation, a great multitude of people from every tribe, tongue, and nation will come to Christ. It is likely they will be martyred too, because of the depiction of the great multitude worshipping God before the throne in Revelation 7.

Jesus was the person who opened all of the seals; six of them at this point. After the sixth seal was broken, there was a pause in the story in which an angel was given authority to seal 12,000 people from each of the 12 tribes of Israel for a total of 144,000 people. Being sealed meant no one could touch them.

Teaching

Revelation 8:1–6: Wiersbe noted that the first six verses depict a time of preparation.[1] Jesus opened the seventh seal, and heaven was quiet for "about half an hour" (v. 1). The quietness of heaven is similar to the calm before the storm. Everything that will happen from here isn't that great for the people of earth.

Seven angels were given seven trumpets (v. 2). The heavenly silence was broken by an angel who stood before the altar with a gold incense burner that was offered "with the prayers of all the saints" (v. 3). The angel offered the prayers "in the presence of God" (v. 4) before filling the incense burner with fire and throwing it to the earth (v. 5). As a result, there were "rumblings of thunder, flashes of lightning, and an earthquake" (v. 5). Remember, prior to this the 144,000 had to be sealed.

Revelation 8:7: Four trumpets were blown in the remainder of chapter 8. Trumpets normally served as a warning, an announcement of an incoming army, the pronouncement of a new king, or the coming of the Year of Jubilee.

At the first trumpet, "Hail and fire, mixed with blood, were hurled to the earth" (v. 7). As a result, "A third of the earth was burned up, a third of the trees were burned up, and all of the green grass was burned up" (v. 7). Wiersbe characterized this as a judgment on the earth.[2] *Nelson's Commentary* pointed out that this was a combination of the first and the seventh plagues in Exodus.[3]

Revelation 8:8–11: At the second trumpet, "Something like a great mountain ablaze with fire was hurled into the sea" (v. 8). As a result, "A third of the sea became blood, a third of the living creatures in the sea died, and a third of the ships were destroyed" (vv. 8–9). Wiersbe characterized this as a judgment on the seas.[4] At the third trumpet, "a great star, blazing like a torch, fell from heaven" on a third of the "rivers and springs of water" (v. 10). This star was named "Wormwood." As a result, "A third of the waters became wormwood. Many of the people died from the waters, because they had been made bitter" (v. 11). MacArthur notes that "Wormwood" was "a bitter, poisonous substance from a root that

[1] Warren W. Wiersbe, *The Bible Exposition Commentary: Ephesians–Revelation* (Colorado Springs: David C. Cook, 1989), 592.

[2] Wiersbe, 593.

[3] Earl Radmacher, Ronald B. Allen, and H. Wayne House, *Nelson's New Illustrated Bible Commentary* (Nashville: Thomas Nelson, 1999), 1746.

[4] Wiersbe, 593.

causes drunkenness and eventually death."[5] Wiersbe characterized this as a judgment on fresh waters.[6]

Revelation 8:12–13: At the fourth trumpet, "A third of the sun was struck, a third of the moon, and a third of the stars, so that a third of them were darkened" (v. 12). As a result, "A third of the day was without light, and the night as well" (v. 12). In verse 13, after the fourth trumpet, a talking eagle flew overhead and pronounced woe "to those who live on the earth, because of the remaining trumpet blasts that the three angels are about to sound!"

Closing

The seventh seal has now been broken. In this process, the prayers of the saints, a heavenly offering, has been hurled at the earth. Angels sounded their trumpets in warning at God's judgments that would fall to the earth.

In response, we should urgently share the good news of Jesus so that people might repent and avoid the coming judgment.

The Daily Word

The seventh seal brought half an hour of silence in the throne room of heaven, and an angel offered incense and the prayers of the saints in the presence of God. John's vision continued as the first four angels blew the first four trumpets. The trumpets brought forth havoc on earth—fires destroying a third of the earth, a third of the sea filling with blood, a third of all freshwater becoming bitter, followed by darkness covering a third of the sun, moon, and stars. Finally, an eagle cried out in warning: "Woe! Woe! Woe!" Things were about to get *even worse* with the three remaining trumpets.

Do you find it difficult to imagine living through the images in John's vision? Yes, the reality is you could possibly experience this turmoil, even as a follower of Christ. However, even in the face of *darkness*, even in the face of *turmoil*, even in the face of *destruction, the Lord promises His presence.* He is your protector, and He is your hope. No matter what you will face—darkness, bitter water, or fire—the Lord promises to never forsake you. He is in your midst. He will be your strength when you are weak. Today, share the Lord's promises so others can find security, even in the midst of turmoil. Go!

---

[5] John MacArthur, *The MacArthur Bible Commentary* (Nashville: Thomas Nelson, 2005), 2009–10.

[6] Wiersbe, 593.

I looked again and heard an eagle flying high overhead, crying out in a loud voice, "Woe! Woe! Woe to those who live on the earth, because of the remaining trumpet blasts that the three angels are about to sound!"
—Revelation 8:13

Further Scripture: Deuteronomy 31:6; Proverbs 18:10; Revelation 8:1–2

Questions

1. The opening of the seventh seal was immediately followed by what (Revelation 8:1)? Do you think that during this period of silence, the incense and prayers of all the saints were going up before God? If so, why is that significant before anything happened after the seventh seal was opened?

2. Why do you think the angel filled the censer with the fire of the altar and threw it to earth? What are your thoughts about the peals of thunder, flashes of lightning, and an earthquake (Revelation 8:5; 11:19; 16:18)?

3. What judgment did the first trumpet bring to the earth?

4. With the second trumpet, something like a burning mountain was thrown into the sea. Do you think this might be a reference to the Mediterranean Sea, which John would have known, or is it more likely "oceans"? What do you think "Wormwood" means in this context (Revelation 8:11)?

5. What proportion of the earth is affected with each of the first four trumpets? Did John record any repentance by the people up to this point?

6. What did the Holy Spirit highlight to you in Revelation 8 through the reading or the teaching?

Lesson 9: Revelation 9

I AM: The Fifth and Sixth Trumpets

Teaching Notes

Intro

We continue our study of Revelation in chapter 9. The book's title is Revelation, not Revelations, because it is one continuous vision given by Jesus Christ to His apostle, John. Chapter 1 explains about the revelation, and chapters 2—3 cover the seven churches of Asia. Chapters 4—5 cover the throne room of God getting ready for the Lamb. Chapters 6—8 give a picture of how Christ will show up to His people—both Jews, Gentiles, and unbelievers. Based on all our research, here's our understanding of the chronology of this:

1. Seven years while Jesus unpacks the seven scrolls, releasing the Antichrist and then war, famine, death, the waiting martyred, catastrophic natural events, and silence.

2. The last three and a half years of this seven is the period of the Great Tribulation. The Tribulation begins when the Antichrist goes into the third temple (the Abomination of Desolation) and declares he is god.

3. After a pause, seven trumpets (angels) are revealed who warn about coming dangers. We've looked at the first four: (1) fires, (2) seas polluted through blood, (3) contaminated fresh water, (4) and the sun, moon, and stars damaged as nature changes.

We pick up with the fifth and sixth sounding trumpets in chapter 9.

Teaching

Revelation 9:1–2: After the fifth trumpet has been blown, a star will fall from the skies and be given a key to the shaft of the abyss (v. 1). The star, based on verse 11, could be a demon or Satan himself, or a third possibility could be an angel.[1] Kyle leans toward Satan. Other biblical passages support this:

---

[1] John MacArthur, *The MacArthur Bible Commentary* (Nashville: Thomas Nelson, 2005), 2010.

1. Luke 10:18 records Jesus' words to the 70: "I watched Satan fall from heaven like a lighting flash."
2. Isaiah 14:12–14 states: "Shining morning star, how you have fallen from the heavens! You destroyer of nations, you have been cut down to the ground" (Isaiah 14:12).
3. Ezekiel 28:12–15 states: "From the day you were created you were blameless in your ways until wickedness was found in you" (Ezekiel 28:15).

This means Satan received a key, opened the shaft to the bottomless pit, and the smoke came up from a great furnace (v. 2). Many scholars think this means Satan will release the demonic host in the abyss, bringing hell to earth.[2] So some refer to the fifth trumpet as the demonic invasion. Regardless of who opens the abyss—Satan, a demon, or an angel, the demonic host is given one more chance to do their worst.

Revelation 9:3–6: Next, locusts came out of the smoke, and they were given the same power that scorpions have (v. 3). MacArthur states, "These are not normal locusts, however, but specially prepared ones that are merely the outward form of demons, who, like locusts, will bring swarming desolation."[3] The locusts were told not to harm the grass, because it was already destroyed, but only those who do not have God's seal on their foreheads (v. 4). This would be everyone except the 144,000 who have God's seal on their foreheads. They were not permitted to kill but only torment their victims for five months (v. 5). MacArthur explains the normal life cycle of a locust is five months, usually from May to September.[4] The torment would become so bad that people will unsuccessfully attempt suicide to escape it (v. 6).

Revelation 9:7–12: The locusts looked like horses equipped for battle with gold crowns and men's faces, hair like women's hair, teeth like lions, and chests like iron breastplates. Their wings sounded like chariots rushing into battle (vv. 7–9), and their tails had stingers like scorpions (v. 10). Some scholars suggest these locusts were from the demonic and also had a hierarchy within the demonic just like there is a hierarchy within angels. MacArthur states that demonic creatures have a king whose name in "both Greek and Hebrew means 'destroyer.' Apparently, 'the angel of the bottomless pit' is one of Satan's most trusted leaders or, possibly, Satan himself."[5] This is a picture of all-out satanic warfare.

---

[2] MacArthur, 2010.

[3] MacArthur, 2010.

[4] MacArthur, 2010.

[5] MacArthur, 2010.

Don't forget that Jesus will still be in control, and He will allow this (Ephesians 6:12). I think we deal with this today. John 10:10 says Satan "comes only to steal and to kill and to destroy." Verse 12 warns that there are two more "woes" (trumpets) to come.

Revelation 9:13–21: The sixth angel blows his trumpet, and John heard a voice come from the four horns of the gold altar that is before God (v. 13). This language is of the mercy seat. The voice instructs the sixth angel to release the four angels who are bound at the Euphrates River (v. 14). These are also fallen angels who were prepared for the exact moment to be released to lead an army to kill one-third of the human race (v. 15). Two hundred million demonic troops will be involved (v. 16). The army horsemen wore breastplates that were red, blue, and yellow, and the horses' heads were lions' heads that breathed out fire, smoke, and sulfur (v. 17).

A third of the human race would be killed by these three plagues—fire, smoke, and sulfur (v. 18). Revelation 6:8 describes a fourth of the human race being destroyed, so added to this third, over half of the human race will be gone at this point. The horses have tails, which resemble snakes that inflict injury (v. 19). Those who were not killed STILL DID NOT REPENT and continued to worship demons and idols (v. 20). "They did not repent of their murders, their sorceries, their sexual immorality, or their thefts" (v. 21).

Closing

The reason for all of this is to call people to repent. Half of the world's population has been killed, yet, people still do not turn to God.

The Daily Word

When the fifth trumpet sounded, smoke covered the earth, bringing darkness. Locusts with the power of scorpions were told not to harm the grass but *only harm people who did not have God's seal on their foreheads.* They were not permitted to kill but only torment for five months. The people wanted to die, but death would flee them. The sixth trumpet brought death to a third of the human race as a demonic invasion of 200 million mounted troops were sent out, bringing more fire, smoke, and sulfur.

Torment and death came upon people who did not repent of their disobedience to God. However, even in the final days, *people will have the opportunity to turn and repent.* Why wait? *Choose to turn to the Lord today!* Perhaps you know some who haven't given their lives to Jesus. Pray for them, fast for them, share and model God's love so they will want to know the Jesus in you. The woes will come, the pain will come, and it will be miserable. Today, share with someone the hope you have in Jesus, despite difficult circumstances. Jesus promises hope, peace, and eternal love to all those who believe and repent of their wicked ways.

They were told not to harm the grass of the earth, or any green plant, or any tree, but only people who do not have God's seal on their foreheads. They were not permitted to kill them but were to torment them for five months; their torment is like the torment caused by a scorpion when it strikes a man. In those days people will seek death and will not find it; they will long to die, but death will flee from them. —Revelation 9:4–6

Further Scripture: Luke 24:47; Acts 26:20; Revelation 9:20–21

Questions

1. In Revelation 9:1, who do you think the star that fell from heaven was (Isaiah 14:12; Luke 10:18; Revelation 8:10; 20:1)? Why do you think that?

2. In Revelation 9:3, who or what do the locusts represent? What prophet in Scripture may have foretold this day (Exodus 10:4–5; Joel 2:2, 3; Revelation 9:10)?

3. According to Revelation 9:2–3, why would God release demons to torment people on earth (Exodus 12:23; Revelation 7:2–3)? How bad do you think it will actually be (Job 3:21; Revelation 6:16)?

4. According to Revelation 9:14–15, how many people on earth will be killed? At this time, how many have been killed in all as a result of God's great judgments (Revelation 6:7–8)?

5. Do the people who are left repent after seeing so much death? What does this say about the severity and perversity of evil during this time on earth? Do you think we are living in this time now? Are we any more evil than the people that lived in ancient times, like in the days of Noah (Genesis 6:5; 13:13)? Why do you think God has held back His wrath this long (2 Peter 3:3–10)?

6. What did the Holy Spirit highlight to you in Revelation 9 through the reading or the teaching?

Lesson 10: Revelation 10

I AM: The Mighty Angel and the Small Scroll

Teaching Notes

Intro

We've now covered John's vision of six of seven angels who blow trumpets. Right before the trumpets blew, 144,000 people, 12,000 from each tribe of Israel who were Jewish evangelists, were sealed by God so they would not be harmed by anything to come. Chapter 10 presents an interlude between the sixth and seventh trumpets. Remember there was also an interlude between the sixth and seventh seals.

So far six trumpets (angels) have revealed warnings about coming dangers: (1) fires; (2) polluted seas through blood; (3) contaminated fresh water; (4) the sun, moon, and stars damaged as nature changes; (5) the demonic invasion that torments those who don't have the seal for five months; and (6) 200,000,000 demons in the form of an army of locusts wage war. After the sixth trumpet, over half of the world's living population will be destroyed. According to Revelation 6:8, one-third of the population had already been destroyed, so at this point, over one-half of the world's population is gone. This leads into the pause of chapter 10.

Teaching

Revelation 10:1: In verse 1, John saw another mighty angel coming down from heaven in a cloud with a rainbow over his head. MacArthur points out that "another" mighty angel identifies another created being, not Jesus, and describes the angel as "filled with splendor, greatness, and strength."[1]

Look at the angels already presented in Revelation:

1. Revelation 5:2 also proclaims the presence of "a mighty angel" asking who was worthy of opening the seals. The answer was Jesus.

---

[1] John MacArthur, *The MacArthur Bible Commentary* (Nashville: Thomas Nelson, 2005), 2010.

2. An angel is described as having "great authority coming down from heaven" in Revelation 18:1.

3. In Revelation 12:7, the angel there is identified as Michael.

About the angel in Revelation 10:1, *Nelson's Commentary* explains, "It is unlikely that this is Michael, who is referred to by name elsewhere (Revelation 12:7, Daniel 12:1), or Christ, since He is never called an angel in the New Testament."[2] In Exodus 16:10, a cloud appeared, revealing God's glory. The language of Revelation 10:1 is similar.

Revelation 10:2–3: The bottom line is that no one knows who this angel will be. The angel has a little scroll open in his hand, and he puts his right foot on the sea and his left foot on the land (v. 2). I wonder if this is the same scroll that was opened with the seven seals. If it were that scroll, then this angel is Christ. The angel cried out like a roaring lion and seven thunders spoke with their voices (v. 3).

Revelation 10:4: John was ready to write down what the seven thunders said, but a voice from heaven told him not to (v. 4). Revelation 1:4 spoke of seven Spirits of God, but we cannot tell if these seven thunders are the same Spirits. *Nelson's Commentary* explains that the voice from heaven is different from the mighty angel and is probably Christ.[3]

Revelation 10:5–7: The angel who stood with one foot on the sea and one on the land then raised his right hand to heaven and swore an oath to the Eternal God and Creator of all things. The angel swore, "There will no longer be an interval of time, but in the days of the sound of the seventh angel, when he will blow his trumpet, then God's hidden plan will be completed as He announced to His servants the prophets" (vv. 5–7). *Nelson's Commentary* states, "After the sounding of the seventh trumpet, there will be 'no more delay' in the unfolding of events leading toward Christ's return."[4]

When I read verse 7, I think this is exactly what we set out to do in revive-SCHOOL. MacArthur says verse 7 explains, "The mystery [or hidden plan] is the final consummation of all things as God destroys sinners and establishes His righteous kingdom on earth. This mystery, though not fully revealed, was declared to God's prophets (Amos 3:7)."[5]

---

[2] Earl D. Radmacher, Ronald B. Allen, and H. Wayne House, eds., *Nelson's New Illustrated Bible Commentary* (Nashville: Thomas Nelson, 1999), 1748.

[3] Radmacher et al., 1748.

[4] Radmacher et al., 1748–49.

[5] MacArthur, 2012.

God's plan will then be complete. MacArthur points out that the Greek term for mystery or hidden means "to shut" or "to close." That means everything that has been shut or closed will now be open (Ephesians 3:4–5).

The value of the oath is huge because it promises that all will come to fruition. Our key verse for all of reviveSCHOOL is Matthew 5:17: "Don't assume that I came to destroy the Law or the Prophets. I did not come to destroy but to fulfill." This whole mystery—this whole plan—will come to fruition.

Revelation 10:8–11: The voice from heaven spoke again and told John to take the scroll from the angel's hand. John did as he was instructed, and the angel then told John to eat the scroll that would be bitter in his stomach (bitter to swallow) but sweet as honey in his mouth (vv. 8–9).

The scroll shows the contradiction of what is to come. What is to come will not be good because people will be hurt in the process, but it will be good because of the fulfillment of God's plan. God's Word is described as bread (Matthew 4:4), as milk (1 Peter 2:2), as a delight (Jeremiah 15:16), as meat by the Apostle Paul, and as honey in Psalms. In Ezekiel 2:9, the scroll was fed to Ezekiel.

John took the scroll and ate it. It was sweet like honey in his mouth but bitter in his stomach (v. 10). Then he was told he "must prophesy again about many peoples, nations, languages, and kings" (v. 11).

Closing

Sometimes when the Word of God is released, people don't like it because it tastes bitter. If you don't believe Jesus died on the cross for your sins and that He is coming back, then you are going to hell. That's a bitter message for unbelievers. Unbelievers will face eternal destruction. But if you believe Jesus died on the cross and came back to life to be your Lord and Savior, then you can have hope eternal in this entire process.

The oath is that everything we've talked about through our entire study of the Bible is coming to fruition. We haven't even gotten to the seventh trumpet yet when all this is released. John was given a message of warning to tell everyone.

The Daily Word

Before the seventh trumpet was blown, John saw a mighty angel coming down from heaven surrounded by a cloud. When the angel cried out, seven thunders spoke, but a voice told John not to write it down. Then the angel announced there would no longer be an interval of time—no more delay, the wait is over. When the seventh angel blew the seventh trumpet, *then God's hidden plan, His mystery, will be completed.*

As you read these words and this vision of John, trust a time will come when the mystery of the gospel and of Christ will be fully revealed. The time will come when the wait is over, and the plan is completed. Until then the Lord will provide you the strength and motivation to reveal truth. The Lord will provide grace to share about the mysteries of Christ and the fullness and the riches of His glory. The time to turn away from evil ways, to repent, and to seek the Lord *is now*. May any hesitation and pause in receiving Christ in your life cease, so when Christ does return, and His plan is completed—you are ready!

There will no longer be an interval of time, but in the days of the sound of the seventh angel, when he will blow his trumpet, then God's hidden plan will be completed, as He announced to His servants the prophets.
—Revelation 10:6–7

Further Scripture: 1 Corinthians 2:7; Ephesians 3:8–9; Revelation 10:10–11

Questions

1. In Revelation 10:1, what do you think the rainbow on the head of the angel represents?

2. In Revelation 10:4, God told John not to write down what he heard from the seven peals of thunder. How hard do you think it was for John to keep this to himself? Do you believe there are people today who may know a word from the Lord and aren't privileged to share it?

3. Read Revelation 10:7. What do you think this means? What is the mystery of God? Will all Bible prophecy be fulfilled at this time?

4. The angel instructed John to eat the "little book." Where else in Scripture do you see this (Ezekiel 2:8–9; 3:1–3)? What do you think Revelation 10:9 means? Why is the little book sweet tasting to his mouth but sour to his stomach?

5. What did the Holy Spirit highlight to you in Revelation 10 through the reading or the teaching?

Lesson 11: Revelation 11

I AM: The Two Witnesses

Teaching Notes

Intro

As we study through Revelation, our hope is that you are pressing into the Scripture for yourself and allowing the Lord to teach you. Remember, the angel took an oath saying that "there will no longer be an interval of time" when the seventh angel blew his trumpet, but that "God's hidden plan will be completed" (Revelation 10:6–7). The bride of Christ needs to be ready for His return.

Up to this point, six trumpets have been sounded. Revelation 10 depicts a pause between the sixth and the seventh blasts. It was almost as if God was setting the table for the final act. Revelation 11 begins with a step back in the timeline of the book. Two witnesses will be described who will prophesy for 1,260 days. Some argue that the witnesses prophesying began at the beginning of the seven-year tribulation. Our position is that the witnesses prophesy during the Great Tribulation, the second half of the seven-year period.

Teaching

Revelation 11:1–3: The sanctuary and the altar John was told to measure could be the third temple. A third temple has to be standing at this time because the Antichrist will reveal himself at the Lord's temple where sacrifices are being made. John was commanded to not measure the courtyard of the temple "because it is given to the nations, and they will trample the holy city for 42 months" (v. 2). Forty-two months is another way of saying three and a half years.

Throughout the Great Tribulation, Jerusalem will be given to the nations. The Antichrist established a peace agreement during the first three and a half years, so things had been pretty quiet. Daniel prophesied about this time: "He will make a firm covenant with many for one week, but in the middle of the week he will put a stop to sacrifice and offering. And the abomination of desolation will be on a wing of the temple until the decreed destruction is poured out on the desolator" (Daniel 9:27). One week in Daniel depicted seven years.

Revelation 11:4: At the same time of this shift, God will establish two witnesses to prophesy: "These are the two olive trees and the two lampstands that stand before the Lord of the earth" (v. 4). This was a reference to Zechariah 3—4. MacArthur noted that the oil in the lamps came from olive trees.[1] The olive trees and the lampstands are pictures of revival. Their inclusion sparks a message of repentance.

In Zechariah, Joshua and Zerubbabel were described as the olive trees and the lampstands because they rebuilt the temple. Now, these two new witnesses will do the same thing during the second half of the Tribulation by pointing people to the Lord and warning that His judgment is coming.

Revelation 11:5–6: God will protect the witnesses in miraculous ways. Fire will come out of their mouths to consume anyone who tries to harm them (v. 5). They also are given the power to keep it from raining, to turn the water to blood, "and to strike the earth with every plague whenever they want" (v. 6).

Who are the witnesses? MacArthur listed six reasons why they could be Moses and Elijah:

1. "Like Moses, they will strike the earth with plagues, and like Elijah, they have the power to keep it from raining."
2. "Jewish tradition expected both Moses and Elijah to return."
   - According to Deuteronomy 18:15, "The Lord your God will raise up for you a prophet like me from among your own brothers. You must listen to him."
   - Malachi 4:5 states, "Look, I am going to send you Elijah the prophet before the great and awesome Day of the Lord comes."
   - John 1:21 states, "'What then?' they asked him. 'Are you Elijah?' 'I am not,' he said. 'Are you the Prophet?' 'No,' he answered."
   - The Jewish people were constantly waiting for and expecting Moses and Elijah to return.
3. "Both Moses and Elijah were present at the transfiguration."
4. "Both Moses and Elijah used supernatural means to provoke repentance."
5. "Elijah was taken up into Heaven alive and God buried Moses' body where it would never be found."
6. The length of the drought the two witnesses bring is the same as that brought by Elijah.[2]

---

[1] John MacArthur, *The MacArthur Bible Commentary* (Nashville: Thomas Nelson, 2005), 2013.

[2] MacArthur, 2013.

The witnesses will bring a message of judgment but also the gracious possibility of mercy.

Revelation 11:7–10: In verse 7, the phrase, "When they finish their testimony," implies the ending of the three and a half years. The beast, which represents the presence of Satan, "comes up out of the abyss" and "will make war with them, conquer them, and kill them" (v. 7). Some believe that this occurs at the ending of the first three and a half years, while others hold that this occurs later. The critical detail is the timing of the beast coming up out of the abyss. It is difficult to determine with certainty the exact placement of this event on the timeline.[3]

After the beast killed the witnesses, he left their bodies to rot "in the public square of the great city, which is prophetically called Sodom and Egypt, where also their Lord was crucified" (v. 8). That city was Jerusalem. People would come by to see the bodies for three and a half days. No one would be permitted to bury them during this time. The world will rejoice over the death of the witnesses and will "send gifts to one another because these two prophets brought judgment to those who live on the earth" (v. 10).

Revelation 11:11–14: After three and a half days, God raised them from the dead (v. 11). God called the witnesses to heaven in a cloud "while their enemies watched them" (v. 12). As this happened, an earthquake struck the city and "a tenth of the city fell, and 7,000 people were killed in the earthquake" (v. 13). Those remaining "were terrified and gave glory to the God of heaven" (v. 13). Now, "the second woe has passed" (v. 14). We have still been in the interlude between the sixth and seventh trumpet.

Revelation 11:15–19: Now, the seventh trumpet was blown and voices in heaven proclaimed the victory and everlasting kingdom of the Messiah (v. 15). The 24 elders worshipped God (vv. 17–18).

Closing

God's faithfulness, power, and wrath are going to be revealed. God's mercy and faithfulness will also be revealed as the seventh trumpet leads into the seven bowls of God's wrath. This was all started by the work of the two witnesses.

The Daily Word

During the tribulation brought by the first six trumpets, the Lord empowered two witnesses to prophesy for 1,260 days, or three and a half years. As the two

---

[3] MacArthur, 2013.

witnesses finished their testimony, the beast from the abyss, a presence of Satan, killed them. However, after three and a half days, God's breath of life restored them, and *they were resurrected to heaven.* Then the seventh angel blew his trumpet and loud voices in heaven proclaimed victory: "The kingdom of the world has become the kingdom of our Lord and of His Messiah, and He will reign forever and ever!" People were terrified *but gave God glory.*

The two witnesses brought a *picture of revival during the tribulation.* They had the power of the Resurrected Savior *in them.* You have this same power of the Resurrected Savior in *you.* You are a treasured vessel to be used for His glory. God gave you authority over darkness, over demons, and over sickness because of His power alive in you. He promises to give you everything you need to be a witness so people will be saved from eternal judgment. Today, *go* and proclaim the good news in the power and authority of the Lord.

The 24 elders, who were seated before God on their thrones, fell facedown and worshiped God, saying: We thank You, Lord God, the Almighty, who is and who was, because You have taken Your great power and have begun to reign. —Revelation 11:16–17

Further Scripture: Luke 9:1; Romans 8:11; Revelation 11:6

Questions

1. What did God command John to do at the beginning of Revelation 11? Why was he to exclude the courtyard outside the temple? To what temple did the angel refer (Daniel 9:27; Luke 21:24; 2 Thessalonians 2:4)?

2. How long will two witnesses prophesy? How were they described? What kind of authority will they have?

3. How were the two witnesses similar to Elijah and Moses (Exodus 7–11; 1 Kings 17; Malachi 4:5; James 5:16b–18; Revelation 11:5–6)?

4. How will the two witnesses be killed? How long will they be dead? What will the people's reaction be when they die? What will their reaction be after the witnesses have risen?

5. The most reliable Greek manuscripts omit the phrase "Who is to come," in Revelation 11:17. Why is that phrase not needed (Revelation 1:4, 8; 4:8)?

6. What did the Holy Spirit highlight to you in Revelation 11 through the reading or the teaching?

Lesson 12: Revelation 12

I AM: The Great Dragon

Teaching Notes

Intro

We are plowing through the book of Revelation, the 10th and final section of reviveSCHOOL. It's crazy that we have been doing this for two years! The book of Revelation is the revelation of Christ. Christ is coming back, so you and I can have hope. Typically, when thinking of the book of Revelation, one is afraid of the scary end times. However, the book of Revelation should really bring you hope, a sense of peace, and victory. The word for this book is *I AM*. Christ is the beginning and the end. We have nothing to fear because Christ is in control. In this chapter, we are going to see a transition into the seven signs. Chapter 12 takes place after the seventh trumpet.

Teaching

Revelation 12:1–2: The heaven discussed here is the third heaven—the heaven in the presence of the Lord. In the course of the book of Revelation, there are seven signs. These signs are both divine and demonic. There are many different theories as to who the woman described here is. Some believe she represents the church; some say she represents believing Jews; others say she represents the ethnic Jews. I believe she is the representation of Israel. Throughout the Old Testament, Israel was referred to as a woman or a wife of God.

There are other women mentioned in Revelation: Jezebel (2:20), the scarlet woman (17:3–6), and the wife of the Lamb (19:7). I am bringing them up because of the images used in Revelation. As you read through this book, you have to use Scripture to discern who or what the Scriptures are talking about. Comparing the Scripture to the other women mentioned leads me to believe that the pregnant woman described is the nation of Israel. The first sign is a pregnant lady.

Revelation 12:3–4: Picture this: a pregnant woman is about to give birth and then a dragon enters the picture. This is the second sign. The dragon has seven heads and 10 horns. This dragon is the woman's mortal enemy. The whole purpose of the dragon is to devour the Child. The dragon is representative of Satan. The dragon's tail knocked one-third of the stars to earth. Many believe that the stars hurled to the ground represent the angels that joined Satan's rebellion and became demons. One-third of the angel population joined Satan. The entire goal of Satan and his angels is to destroy the pregnant woman, and if not her, her child.

There is a lot of symbolism and language that can be examined, discerned, and debated. The seven heads could be seven nations, seven mountains, or seven kings. I think it is fair to say that whatever the seven are, the Antichrist will be involved with them. The whole goal of the Antichrist is to go after the child.

Revelation 12:5–6: The woman (Israel) gave birth to a son. The son is Jesus. Jesus is delivered from the dragon and is enthroned in heaven. This is a beautiful picture of His ascension. Also, compare this picture to the birth of Jesus on earth. After Jesus was born, Mary and Joseph were forced to flee to Egypt in order to escape Herod, who was killing baby boys.

The woman fled to the wilderness. We have seen this language before in the book of Exodus. I love this picture because God is constantly taking care of His people in the wilderness. The big questions here are: Where does this event fit? Before the Great Tribulation? Or, is it part of the Great Tribulation? We will get back to these questions later.

Revelation 12:7–9: A war broke out in heaven. Michael, the top angel, and his angles battled against the dragon and his angels/demons. The dragon and his angels/demons were cast out of heaven. There is no question about who the great dragon is. John wrote that he is called the devil and Satan. He is the deceiver of the whole world.

Satan was thrown out of heaven onto the earth. We get this picture of Satan just hanging out and messing around on earth. He is known as god of this world. Even though Satan and his demons were thrown out of heaven they still have access to it (Job 1:6). We have the imagery that Satan is going back and forth from heaven to earth. *Nelson's Commentary* states, "The devil's expulsion from heaven to the earth means that this world becomes his base of operations."[1]

Revelation 12:10–12: Nelson's Commentary explains that Satan was conquered three times: "by the blood of the Lamb, . . . the word of their testimony, . . . and the martyrdom of some of the brethren."[2] While here on earth, Satan will do anything to kill, steal, and destroy. He knows he is on borrowed time. Satan cannot win against Christ.

---

[1] Earl D. Radmacher, Ronald B. Allen, and H Wayne House, eds., *Nelson's New Illustrated Bible Commentary* (Nashville: Thomas Nelson, 1999), 1752.

[2] Radmacher et al., 1752.

Revelation 12:13–14: Israel will continually and constantly be attacked by Satan as the seed of the Messiah came from Israel. The goal of the dragon at this point is to prolong his time on earth by keeping Jesus from coming back.

The image we have in this passage is that in the first three and a half years, we have the attack against the pregnant woman. During the second three and half years, the woman is protected from the dragon.

Revelation 12:15–17: Satan is trying to flood the Israelites. Even though the enemy tried to attack them, God saved the Israelites. We do know that over time, there will be a group of Israelites that die. God is going to spare at least one-third of His people.

Satan is frustrated with his war against the woman, so he will go after all the other followers of Christ—those who keep Gods words and do His commands. Satan, the dragon, is ready for battle.

Closing

It is safe to say, that for three and a half years, God is protecting the Israelites and that is why everything else continues to break loose. Join us as we dive in again tomorrow in the book of Revelation 13.

The Daily Word

Two signs appeared to John. First, a pregnant woman was crying out in labor before giving birth. Symbolically, this most likely represents the Messiah's birth in Israel. Second, a fiery red dragon, a symbol of Satan, was standing in front of the pregnant woman, ready to devour her child. The woman gave birth to a son, a male who would shepherd all nations. In the vision, the child was *not devoured by Satan* but rather caught up to God to His throne. In the end, *the dragon did not win the war against the woman*, and he did not gain her baby son. This vision likely illustrates Jesus remaining on the throne and Satan left to wage war against those who have kept God's commands and have the testimony about Jesus.

From the beginning, the enemy has attempted to defeat the plans of God. Even today, victory belongs to the Lord and to His people who keep His commands and hold fast to the testimony of Jesus. Satan seeks to steal, kill, and destroy. Be ready. Stand strong in the battle. You are equipped. *The enemy is defeated by the power of Jesus' name.* Jesus is the Good Shepherd to the nations. Therefore, follow His voice and hold fast to Jesus.

And the dragon stood in front of the woman who was about to give birth, so that when she did give birth he might devour her child. But she gave birth to

> **a Son—a male who is going to shepherd all nations with an iron scepter—and her child was caught up to God and to His throne. —Revelation 12:4–5**
>
> Further Scripture: Genesis 3:15; John 10:10–11; Revelation 12:17

Questions

1. Who is the son that the woman gives birth to (Psalm 2:9; Revelation 12:5)? What people group, then, would the woman symbolize (Romans 1:3; 9:4–5)?

2. Who is depicted as the fiery red dragon (Revelation 12:9; 20:2)? What will be the signal that Satan's reign is over (Revelation 11:15)?

3. What happens at the midpoint of the tribulation (Daniel 9:27; Matthew 24:15; Revelation 11:2)? How does God protect and preserve Israel during this time (Daniel 11:41; Revelation 12:6)?

4. What does Satan know about himself? Who will he specifically target knowing this about himself (Revelation 12:13, 17)?

5. What should you keep doing despite persecution that may come (John 8:31–32)?

6. When the dragon goes off to make war with the rest of the woman's children in Revelation 12:17, do you think these are Jews or Christians (Galatians 4:26, 31; Revelation 13:7)?

7. What did the Holy Spirit highlight to you in Revelation 12 through the reading or the teaching?

Lesson 13: Revelation 13

I AM: The Beast from the Earth and the Sea

Teaching Notes

Intro

It has been a full week. It feels like one ongoing lesson. All of Revelation is John's revelation of *I AM*. Revelation is the restoration of the Garden. It's a beautiful picture. Yesterday's text was the battle between Satan and *The Seed*, which we see over and over again. We already know that the dragon in chapter 12 was Satan. Now we see Satan standing at the sea ready for battle.

Teaching

Revelation 13:1: The very beginning of this chapter transitions from Satan standing on a beach to Satan encountering a different beast, which symbolizes the Antichrist. We are unpacking Satan's plan to use the Antichrist. The word beast means monster.

Revelation 13:2: Satan gave the Antichrist power and authority. This is like a movie. God became flesh through Jesus Christ, and Satan gave authority for flesh called the Antichrist. We are going to break down all the animals listed in the description of the Antichrist. MacArthur wrote that the leopard is "a metaphor for ancient Greece." The bear is "a metaphor for the ancient Medo-Persian Empire." The lion is "a metaphor for the ancient Babylonian Empire."[1] The spirit of the Antichrist could have been present in all of these nations that have tried to conquer the Seed. I do believe that there will be an actual person who is the Antichrist.

   When we talk about the spirit of the Antichrist, we see it described throughout Scripture. In Scripture, the Antichrist is described as a man of sin and lawlessness (2 Thessalonians 2:3–4) and is a prince who is to come (Daniel 9:26). The Antichrist is also described as the little horn (Daniel 7:8), a beast (Revelation 13:2–10,18), and the son of perdition/destruction (John 17:12). He will reign over the Great Tribulation (Daniel 7:25).

---

[1] John MacArthur, *The MacArthur Bible Commentary* (Nashville: Thomas Nelson, 2005), 2017.

MacArthur compared the parallels of Christ and the Antichrist:

	CHRIST	ANTICHRIST
1. Revelation	2 Thessalonians 1:7	2 Thessalonians 2:3, 6, 8
2. Coming	2 Thessalonians 2:1, 8	2 Thessalonians 2:9
3. Message	2 Thessalonians 2:10 (the truth)	2 Thessalonians 2:11 (the lie)
4. Deity	John 1:1 (real)	2 Thessalonians 2:4 (claimed)
5. Authenticating Signs	Acts 2:22	2 Thessalonians 2:9
6. Empowerment	Acts 2:22 (God)	2 Thessalonians 2:9 (Satan)
7. Death	Mark 15:37	Revelation 13:3, 12, 14
8. Resurrection	Mark 16:6	Revelation 13:3, 12, 14[2]

I want to show you that the Antichrist is present in Scripture. You will see different titles and descriptions used throughout. So when you see the dragon and the beast, we begin to see the battle with the woman and all Christ followers.

Revelation 13:3–4: One of the beast's heads appeared dead and then was healed. Many would say this was not a real death. The whole goal of the Antichrist is to parade around as light, tricking people to believing in him. When the Antichrist appears to be healed from a fatal wound, the whole earth will be amazed and begin to follow him. When they follow the beast, they worship the dragon, which is Satan. The world will worship Satan and the beast. They will believe that they are protected by the beast and the dragon.

Revelation 13:5–6: MacArthur wrote, "God will allow him to utter his blasphemies, to bring the reign of Satan to its culmination on earth for three and a half years."[3]

Revelation 13:7: When John wrote "wage war against the saints," there are many opinions on who "the saints" are. Those who take the pretribulation view would argue that the saints are the people who have come to know Christ in the tribulation. No matter what view is taken, there are clearly believers around to wage war against Satan. MacArthur wrote, "The Antichrist will be allowed to massacre

---

[2] MacArthur, 1769.

[3] MacArthur, 2018.

those who are God's children."[4] I'd love to tell you we're going to be pain free and out of here. What if these saints are us? I want us to still be ready. What if we are called to be martyred?

Revelation 13:8–9: Everyone whose name is not written in the Book of Life will be slaughtered. MacArthur explains that the Book of Life is "a divine journal that records the names of all those whom God has chosen to save and who, therefore, are to possess eternal life."[5] Everyone who worshipped the Antichrist will not find their name in the Book of Life.

Revelation 13:10: You have to have a bigger picture here. This is the language of the saints. Are these the believers during the tribulation? Those not raptured? No one can be sure. What if the saints are us? This could be God's plan. Those who are persecuted in the name of Christ are rewarded in heaven (Matthew 5:8). The point is persecution could be coming. I want to see us waiting and prepared.

Revelation 13:11–14: There is the dragon, Satan, and the beast, the Antichrist. And here we see they need help from another beast, who represents the false prophet. His authority will be less than the Antichrist. He is essentially a talking puppet, convincing people to worship the Antichrist. He will attempt to duplicate the signs and miracles of the Messiah and other great prophets.

Revelation 13:15–18: If a person does not worship the Antichrist, they will die. A person has to have the mark of the beast in order to survive. The number will be 666. People have tried to speculate why 666. The only thing I can conclude is that the number six is incomplete. The number six is one number short of God's perfect number seven, thus falling short of perfection. Whether that's accurate, we can't be sure. All we can know is that the number 6 implies not perfect.

Closing

The enemy might have his mark, but praise God, we have ours. It might not be seen on us physically, but it is seen in the physical marks form the crucifixion on Christ. It doesn't matter what all is going down during this time, we know where we are going to be, and we have hope in Him. It is through His death and resurrection that we have the ultimate mark, which is life.

[4] MacArthur, 2018.

[5] MacArthur, 1999.

The Daily Word

As John's vision continued, two more beasts emerged—the antichrist from the sea and a false prophet from the earth. Satan will give the antichrist his power, his throne, and great authority. The false prophet will deceive all those who live on the earth through the signs he performs. The whole earth will be amazed. Many will follow the antichrist and worship him, except those whose names are written in the Book of Life, determined by Jesus the Lamb who was slain for their salvation. Yes, they will continue to worship the Lord. However, they may be destined for captivity and even killed by the sword. *The Lord will grant the saints perseverance and faith.*

In the tribulation, as a believer of Christ, you will possibly face captivity or even be killed by a sword. But as you think of all the possible torture and pain, remember the saints who have gone before you have already experienced persecution for their faith. Because of their pain, others can now live in Christ. In the last days, *the Lord will grant you faith and perseverance.* Remember, Jesus said those who are persecuted for righteousness are blessed and the kingdom of heaven is theirs. So you are to be glad and rejoice because our reward is great in heaven. Today, *rest in the hope from Jesus.* Walk by faith and not with fear. You will be blessed.

All those who live on the earth will worship him, everyone whose name was not written from the foundation of the world in the book of life of the Lamb who was slaughtered. —Revelation 13:8

Further Scripture: Matthew 5:10–12; Colossians 1:11–12; Revelation 13:9–10

Questions

1. Is the sand of the sea in Revelation 13:1 literal or figurative (Revelation 17:15)?

2. What do the "seven heads," "ten horns," and "ten crowns" represent in Revelation 13:1b (Daniel 7:23–25; Revelation 17:10–16)?

3. In your opinion, does Revelation 13:7 speak of saints from before the tribulation or could they be the saints that come to Christ after the start of the tribulation? Why do you think that?

4. How is it that so many on the earth will be completely deceived in the end times when the Bible clearly tells the events? Do you think that there will be believers of Jesus that will be deceived or will some turn their backs on Him during this time (Matthew 24:24)? Why or why not?

5. In Revelation 13:16–18, the mark is described. In our current time, there are companies that are putting chips into people. In your opinion, could this be the start of the marking? Why or why not?

6. What did the Holy Spirit highlight to you in Revelation 13 through the reading or the teaching?

Lesson 14: Revelation 14

I AM: Reaping the Earth's Harvest

Teaching Notes

Intro

This is a brand-new week, and we are still in the book of Revelation. Revelation feels like one long lesson or story that is unfolding. At the end of chapter 13, we saw the Great Tribulation unfold. The Antichrist was given free reign on earth from the Lord. We saw the dragon (Satan), the sea beast (the Antichrist), and the land beast (the false prophet) all working together. We also saw a picture of the saints going through a hard time. Chapter 14 begins to show the end of the Great Tribulation. John changed his viewpoint from the beast to a whole new seed. No more creepy monsters.

Teaching

Revelation 14:1: "The Lamb" referred to in this verse is Jesus. Many biblical scholars have discussed what Mount Zion represents here. *Nelson's Commentary* explains, "Mount Zion is a synonym for earthly Jerusalem, focusing on the hill where the temple was built. There is some difficulty in deciding whether this is a reference to the earthly or heavenly Mount Zion."[1]

Revelation 14:2–3: John saw "The Lamb" but also heard sounds from heaven. This heavenly noise was a new song. It sounds like the 144,000 redeemed from earth are in heaven. These redeemed were the only ones singing.

Revelation 14:4: The 144,000 worshippers of the Lord and elders in heaven are drastically different from the worshippers of the Antichrist who are alive on earth. The 144,000 were the firstfruits for God and the Lamb. *Nelson's Commentary* states, "Firstfruits are the first part of the crop to be gathered, implying a much larger harvest to come later."[2] Jesus modeled this idea better than anyone

---

[1] Earl D. Radmacher, Ronald B. Allen, and H. Wayne House, eds., *Nelson's New Illustrated Bible Commentary* (Nashville: Thomas Nelson, 1999), 1753.

[2] Radmacher et al., 1753.

(1 Corinthians 15:23–26). This is a picture of Christ coming back for more. He is coming back for those who belong to Him.

Revelation 14:5: Many scholars believe this verse means the 144,000 were without sin. I don't believe that is true. We believe Romans 3:23, we are all sinners. *Nelson's Commentary* states, "The 144,000 were not sinless in their earthly lives, but they were without deceit and fault with regard to their testimony for Christ."[3] MacArthur wrote, "The 144,000 speak God's truth accurately and precisely, with no exaggeration or understatement."[4] This is the backdrop of the 144,000. At this point of our reading, they are the representation of the great harvest to come. I believe the Great Tribulation is ending at this point.

Revelation 14:6–7: There is an angel that proclaimed the gospel to the nations. Somehow, everyone hears God's proclamation (Matthew 24:14). The Lord is going to make sure everyone has the chance to hear His good news. We can know God will fulfill His promise. The word "gospel" here means "good news." MacArthur writes that even at this late stage, God continues to urge "the people of the world to change their allegiance from the beast to the Lamb."[5] The angel's message was to give God glory and warn that judgment was coming.

Revelation 14:8: John next described a second angel who followed the first. The first angel brought forth the seven bowls of wrath. *Nelson's Commentary* explains, "Babylon is first mentioned in Revelation here, and it becomes the focus of God's judgment in Revelation 16—18."[6] It represents more than a city; it is an entire world system in rebellion against God.

Revelation 14:9–12: News does not get any better in verse 9. A third angel appeared behind the other two proclaiming, "If anyone worships the beast and his image and receives a mark on his forehead or on his hand, he will also drink the wine of God's wrath" (v. 10). The wrath here is also the wrath of the devil. It is God's wrath, through Satan. The language here is fire and brimstone. Torment will last forever. If you do not embrace the Lamb of God, you will experience torture in hell forever. We cannot afford to be afraid to talk to others about the Lord. The consequences are too great.

---

[3] Radmacher et al., 1754.

[4] John MacArthur, *The MacArthur Bible Commentary* (Nashville: Thomas Nelson, 2005), 2021.

[5] MacArthur, 2021.

[6] Radmacher et al., 1754.

Revelation 14:13: In verse 13, there is another voice John heard from heaven saying, "Write: The dead who die in the Lord from now on are blessed." Remember how we talked about the Beatitudes, the "blessed"? This would be one of them.

Nelson's Commentary basically says, "Hang in there, and you will be blessed at the end."[7] When a believer dies in this context, they will find rest in the Lord. These words are to serve as encouragement to persevere even when times are difficult. Endure until the end. And it looks like we're at the end of the tribulation, according to this text. The gospel had been proclaimed to every person, and the consequence of rejection had been spelled out.

Revelation 14:14: We see in this verse an incredible picture of Christ. The sickle in His hand is a tool for grain harvest. This is the picture of Christ as king. Read Psalm 48:1–2; Isaiah 24:23; and Revelation 19:16. I want to tie in this imagery of Christ coming back as king.

Revelation 14:15–16: A fourth angel appeared crying out that the harvest is ripe—everyone has heard the good news. This was now the best time for everyone to be harvested. With one swing from Christ's sickle, the earth was harvested.

Revelation 14:17–19: A fifth angel appeared who also had a sickle in hand. Then a sixth angel appeared, who had "authority over fire" (v. 18), and tells the fifth angel to use his sickle to gather the ripened grapes from earth. This got drastic really quick. I believe this sickle and the grapes are a representation of judgment. Christ was gathering the harvest, and judgment was being dispensed by the fifth angel.

Revelation 14:20: Many would say this is the battle of Armageddon beginning to take place. This could be the event described in more detail in Revelation 19:11–21. "Outside the city" could be referring to the valley of Jehoshaphat just outside of Jerusalem (Joel 3:12–13).

Closing

Embrace the gospel. Do not embrace the false worship. Embrace Christ. If you do not believe, know that judgment is coming and the blood will begin to flow. The battle of Armageddon will take place, and Christ wins.

---

[7] Radmacher et al., 1755.

The Daily Word

John's vision shifted from the antichrist to the Lamb, and he saw and heard a series of powerful messages from five angels. As the end of the tribulation drew near, messages regarding both salvation and wrath were boldly declared. One message, a voice from heaven, instructed John to write: "The dead who die in the Lord from now on are blessed." And the Spirit responded, "Yes . . . let them rest from their labors, for their works follow them!"

Hang in there, friend. Stay strong in the Lord. None of what you do will be wasted, and in the end, you will be blessed. *Yes,* suffering hurts and open wounds bring pain. *Yes,* the things of this world attempt to satisfy you with temporary pleasures and sweep you away from following Christ fully. *Yes,* trials come along and devastate your heart. And yet, remember, Jesus is victorious. *Jesus is enough.* The Lamb, the One, the Savior of the world came to rescue you from wrath, judgment, and eternal fire. So now, more than ever before, stay strong, and you will be *blessed* because of your perseverance in keeping God's commands and faith in Jesus.

Then I heard a voice from heaven saying, "Write: The dead who die in the Lord from now on are blessed."
"Yes," says the Spirit, "let them rest from their labors, for their works follow them!" —Revelation 14:13

Further Scripture: 1 Peter 4:12–14, 19; Revelation 14:6–7

Questions

1. Who are the 144,000 that are standing on Mount Zion with the Lamb in Revelation 14:1 (Matthew 19:12; Revelation 3:12; 7:4, 13–17)?

2. Do you believe the angel in Revelation 14:6 is there to pronounce judgment on the people on earth, or is he possibly giving them one last appeal to come to Jesus (Daniel 8:19; Acts 14:15)? Why do you think that?

3. According to Revelation 14:9–11, what will happen to those who take the mark of the beast?

4. What is Revelation 14:14–16 talking about (Matthew 13:39–41)? Should faithful followers of Christ fear this?

5. What prophet predicted the horrific event mentioned in Revelation 14:18–20 (Ezekiel 39:17–21)?

6. What did the Holy Spirit highlight to you in Revelation 14 through the reading or the teaching?

Lesson 15: Revelation 15

I AM: Preparation for the Bowl Judgments

Teaching Notes

Intro

Yesterday, we concluded our study of Revelation 14 with the picture of the Son of Man coming on a cloud with a gold crown on His head and a sharp sickle in His hand. He used the sickle over the earth and harvested it. Then, an angel appeared with a sickle, and he used his sickle to gather the grapes of the earth and threw them into the winepress of God's vineyard. Blood flowed out of the winepress up to the horses' bridles for about 180 miles (vv. 14–20). From chapter 14, we go into another weird pause as we study the seven bowls in chapter 15 and the impact of how each was received. It is best to read chapters 6—11 in one sitting to understand the flow.

Teaching

Revelation 15:1–4: John then saw seven angels with the seven last plagues, which will complete God's wrath. "Will be completed" (v. 1) refers to God's plan being fulfilled. There are several views about the tribulation: Some believe Christ's followers will be raptured up to heaven before the tribulation; some believe Christ's followers will be raptured after the seven-year tribulation. Either way, the tribulation will be implemented through six specific seals (Revelation 6):

1. The first horseman on a white horse appears and is the Antichrist. This parallels Matthew 24 to Revelation 6 and is the beginning of the seven-year period of tribulation. The Great Tribulation begins halfway through that seven-year period.

2. A second horseman on a red horse appears to take peace from the people—there will be wars and rumors of wars (Matthew 26).

3. A third horseman on a black horse with a balance scale represents scarcity, inequity, and famine (6:5–6).

4. A fourth horseman on a pale green horse appears who represents death and Hades. (**Note:** Many scholars suggest these first four seals will come early in the first three and a half years of the tribulation, but we don't know for sure.)

5. An altar in heaven appears with faithful martyrs under it (Matthew 24:9; Revelation 6:9–11). We cannot be sure of the timeline of all this, but we can be sure believers will feel the fury during the fifth and sixth seals.

6. An earthquake occurs, the sun turns black, the moon becomes like blood, and a breakdown of all created order begins, announcing that the end of the world is at hand.

Note: Some scholars suggest the seals, the trumpets, and the bowls all happen at the same time. The trumpets proclaimed the coming of (1) raging fires to burn the earth's grasses; (2) pollution of the seas; (3) contamination of the fresh water; and (4) the darkening of a third of the sun, a third of the moon, and a third of the stars. An eagle declared the next three trumpets would call much worse things into action: (5) a demonic invasion; (6) the demons waging war against the people; and (7) the giving of the seven bowls. These actually start the seventh seal. I firmly believe all believers will be raptured before this. At the end of the first half of the seven years, the Great Tribulation begins. Chapter 15 begins with that event.

Wiersbe describes verses 1–4 as, "The Voice of the Victors."[1] Verse 2 describes those who have been victorious against the beast. That victory is seen because they are worshipping in heaven, possibly through martyrdom. The saints are standing on a sea of glass playing God's harps in worship. In Revelation 5:8, the elders are also seen playing harps. MacArthur explains, "There is no sea in heaven (21:1), but the crystal pavement that serves as the floor of God's throne stretches out like a great, glistening sea."[2] These saints "from every nation, including Israel, ultimately triumph over Satan's Antichrist and his system because of their faith in Jesus Christ."[3] The saints will also sing songs of worship (vv. 3–4). Their song describes what they are experiencing—all the nations were, in fact, together in worship of the Lord.

Remember this is an interlude before God's wrath is experienced when the saints are singing in worship. MacArthur points out the song of Moses was "sung by the people of Israel immediately after their passage through the Red Sea and their deliverance from the Egyptian armies (Exodus 15:1–18) . . . of victory and deliverance that the redeemed who overcome Antichrist and his system

---

[1] Warren W. Wiersbe, *The Bible Exposition Commentary: Ephesians–Revelation* (Colorado Springs: David C. Cook, 1989), 608.

[2] John MacArthur, *The MacArthur Bible Commentary* (Nashville: Thomas Nelson, 2005), 2003.

[3] MacArthur, 2023.

will readily identify with."[4] Further, singing the song of Moses and the song of the Lamb mark two "redemptive events: (1) deliverance of Israel by God from Egypt through Moses; and (2) deliverance of sinners by God from sin through Christ."[5]

Revelation 15:5–8: Wiersbe summarizes 15:5—16:21 as, "The Voice of Fulfillment."[6] John watched as the heavenly sanctuary and the ark of the covenant was opened before him (v. 5). Seven angels and seven plagues then came out of the sanctuary dressed in bright linen and gold sashes (v. 6). MacArthur explains, "The [gold] bands demonstrate riches, royalty, and untarnished glory."[7] God is going to reveal who He is!

The living creatures mentioned in verse 7 were introduced in Revelation 4:6b–8—the lion, the calf, the face of a man, and the eagle. One of these creatures gave seven angels seven gold bowls filled with the wrath of God. MacArthur explains the gold bowls "are shallow saucers, familiar items often associated with various functions of the temple worship, such as wine and blood sacrifice. Their flat shallowness pictures how the divine judgments will be emptied instantly, rather than slowly poured, drowning those who refused to drink the cup of salvation"[8] (1 Kings 7:50; 2 Kings 12:13; 25:15). These bowls came straight from the temple.

The sanctuary was filled with smoke from God's glory (Exodus 19:16–18; 40:34–35; 1 Kings 8:10; Isaiah 6:4; Ezekiel 10:4) so that no one could enter it until after the seven plagues were completed (v. 8).

Closing

The presence and wrath of God will be released through seven gold bowls. If you know Jesus, you have nothing to fear from the wrath of God.

The Daily Word

God's wrath is coming to completion—the saints will have endured seven seals and seven trumpets. Now seven angels would distribute the seven bowls of wrath to usher in God's glory. But first the saints celebrated the victory over the beast, his image, and the number of his name as they stood on the sea of glass with harps singing and praising the Lord God Almighty!

---

[4] MacArthur, 2023.

[5] MacArthur, 2023.

[6] Wiersbe, 609.

[7] MacArthur, 2023.

[8] MacArthur, 2024.

John witnessed a victory song after a period of suffering, testing, and tribulation. May this song serve as a reminder to *praise the Lord* and glorify His name throughout your day. You may think you can't carry a tune or keep the rhythm with your toes, but don't let that stop you from *worshipping the Lord* with your heart. Sing Him a new song of praise. Rejoice in the work of His hands. Thank Him for His ways. Recognize His faithful promises and provision in Your life. Whether it's experiencing God answer the impossible or resting in His peace during the mundane, praise Him for victory in His presence. Now go and sing a song to the Lamb of God, Jesus Christ! Who was, and is, and is still to come!

I also saw something like a sea of glass mixed with fire, and those who had won the victory over the beast, his image, and the number of his name, were standing on the sea of glass with harps from God. They sang the song of God's servant Moses and the song of the Lamb: Great and awe-inspiring are Your works, Lord God, the Almighty; righteous and true are Your ways, King of the Nations. —Revelation 15:2–3

Further Scripture: Exodus 15:1; Psalm 98:1; Revelation 15:1

Questions

1. Based on Revelation 15:2–4, do you think at the end the faithful to Christ will be witnesses to the wrath that is going to be poured out on the earth?

2. What did the song of Moses celebrate (Exodus 15)? What does the song of the Lamb celebrate (Jeremiah 10:7; Revelation 5:9; 14:7)?

3. Name some other places in Scripture where God manifests Himself with smoke (Exodus 13:21; 19:18; 33:9; 1 Kings 8:10; Isaiah 6:4)? In this list of references, what was happening? Can you think of other places in Scripture where God's glory is manifested by smoke?

4. What did the Holy Spirit highlight to you in Revelation 15 through the reading or the teaching?

Lesson 16: Revelation 16

I AM: The Seven Bowls

Teaching Notes

Intro

After the seven seals and the seven trumpets, John saw seven bowls that were held by seven angels. This period of time was all about God's wrath. God's wrath was against unbelievers, specifically those individuals who followed the Antichrist.

Teaching

Revelation 16:1–21: John heard a loud voice come from the sanctuary. The sanctuary was in the throne room of heaven. John used multiple senses to totally grasp and understand the images and actions he experienced. Seven angels were commanded to pour out the seven bowls of God's wrath upon the earth.

In verse 2, the first angel poured out a bowl that caused painful sores to break out upon all those who worshipped the image of the beast and wore his mark. Earlier, we saw that those who had the mark of the beast were given access to buying and selling things the believers did not have access to. Now, the mark on their hands or heads meant they would suffer the wrath of God.

MacArthur explains the significance of these specific bowls of wrath: "The Septuagint (LXX) uses the same Greek word to describe the boils that plagued the Egyptians (Exodus 9:9–11) and afflicted Job (Job 2:7). In the New Testament, it describes the open sores that covered the beggar Lazarus (Luke 16:21). All over the world, people will be afflicted with incurable, open, oozing sores."[1] MacArthur adds, "Only the worshippers of the Antichrist will be afflicted (see notes on 13:16; cf. 14:9–11)."[2] The first bowl of wrath was poured out before Christ had come again.

Another angel emptied the second bowl out on the sea. The sea turned into blood, and all the creatures of the sea died. This bowl was similar to the second trumpet. In the sequence of the seals, the trumpets, and now the bowls, the wrath of God seems to have progressively gotten worse. MacArthur explains, "This is

---

[1] John MacArthur, *The MacArthur Bible Commentary* (Nashville: Thomas Nelson, 2005), 2024.

[2] MacArthur, 2024.

reminiscent of the second trumpet (8:8, 9), and of the first plague against Egypt (Exodus 7:20–25)."[3]

In verse 4, the third angel poured out the third bowl. The result of the third bowl being poured was that fresh water rivers and springs turned to blood. All fresh water was turned to blood. There was nothing to drink. The angel of the waters could have been the same angel that poured out the third bowl.

God was described as "who is and who was" from beginning to the end. Verse 6 states the only thing to drink was the blood. The reason was because they brought about the death and destruction of the martyrs.

MacArthur explains, "Verse 6 says that the eternal God will judge justly because they have killed the believers and preachers of the gospel (6:9–11; 7:9–17; 11:18; 17:6; 18:20). This slaughter will have no parallel in history (Matthew 24:21) and neither will the vengeance of God (cf. Romans 12:19–21)."[4] The believers had no water to clean themselves. God's judgment was explained as being fair and proper.

In verse 7, a voice came from the altar and said that the bowls of wrath were justified because God had warned everyone repeatedly that judgment would come. All were given the opportunity to accept Jesus Christ.

The fourth angel poured out the fourth bowl in verse 8. The bowl was poured out on the sun. People were burned. Their flesh was scorched and burned by the fire and the heat. At the end of verse 9, John stated that the people would not repent. These accounts and the people's refusal to repent were similar to Pharaoh's response. The people refused to give God His glory. The people spoke against God. They refused to recognize that God was in control.

Verse 10 gives the account of the fifth bowl. This bowl was poured out on the throne of the beast, and his kingdom was put in darkness. People still blasphemed God even when they realized who the God of heaven was. The result was worldwide darkness.

Bowl six is explained in verse 12. It was poured out on the Euphrates River, and the river was dried up for the kings to be able to cross. MacArthur explains, "Called 'the great river' five times in Scripture, it flows some 1,800 miles from its source on the slopes of Mount Ararat to the Persian Gulf. It forms the eastern boundary of the land God promised to Israel (Genesis 15:18; Deuteronomy 1:7, 11:24; Joshua 1:4; Revelation 9:14)."[5]

MacArthur goes on to explain: "With its flow already reduced by the prolonged drought and intensified heat, God supernaturally will dry it up

---

[3] MacArthur, 2024.

[4] MacArthur, 2024.

[5] MacArthur, 2025.

to make way for the eastern confederacy to reach Israel (Isaiah 11:15)."[6] God cleared a way for all the armies to get to this place so that they would be there for the battle of Armageddon for their own destruction. "The reason for coming may be to rebel against Antichrist; whose failure to alleviate the world's suffering will no doubt erode his popularity. Or, this may be a final act of rabid anti-Semitism intent on destroying Israel, perhaps in retaliation for the plagues sent by her God."[7]

In verse 13, three unclean spirits came from the mouth of the dragon. The three images were of the Antichrist, Satan, and the false prophet. They represent spirits of demons. MacArthur states the language of the "unholy trinity" was to gather the people together for the final battle of Armageddon.[8]

The bowls of wrath were still in the process of coming. But, in verse 15, God emphasized the need to be ready for Christ's return. The image was that of a soldier ready for battle.

The seventh angel poured out his bowl into the air. According to MacArthur, "The voice from the temple in heaven is undoubtedly that of God Himself. 'It is done!' is best translated, 'It has been and will remain done' (cf. John 19:30). God will punctuate the completion of His wrath with a devastating earthquake—the most powerful in earth's history (cf. vv. 18–21)."[9] This reflected a comparison between Jerusalem and Babylon.

Closing

Christ has still not come back yet. The way to avoid being at this end time occurrence is to accept Christ as Savior and Lord.

The Daily Word

The time came for the seven angels to pour out the seven bowls of wrath on the earth, to people with the mark of the beast and those who worshipped his image. Indeed, these people had not repented, had not turned to the Lord, did not bring God glory, and blasphemed His name. Now they would receive God's promised wrath and judgment: painful sores, blood in the sea, blood in the fresh water, burning fire and heat, darkness, lightning, thunder, earthquakes, and 100-pound hail stones. Even still, in the midst of torture, they continued to blaspheme the Lord God Almighty and refused to repent.

---

[6] MacArthur, 2025.

[7] MacArthur, 2025.

[8] MacArthur, 2025.

[9] MacArthur, 2026.

Don't delay repenting and giving your life to Jesus. If you have something hidden, just stop. Let it go. Repent and say: "Lord, forgive me of my sins. I give You my life." There is no sin, no mess, and no ugly situation too far beyond God's love for you. Let your pride go. For once in your life, humble yourself, repent, and receive God's grace. *You will never fully understand His love for you until you let go of control and let His love come into your life.* Give it up and stop running from the Lord. His goodness and mercy will be with you all the days of your life.

And people were burned by the intense heat. So they blasphemed the name of God, who had the power over these plagues, and they did not repent and give Him glory. —Revelation 16:9

Further Scripture: Acts 3:19–20; 2 Corinthians 6:2; Revelation 16:1–2

Questions

1. Briefly describe the plagues of the seven bowls.
2. What will the people's reaction be toward these plagues? Why do you think they will react that way (James 4:6; 2 Peter 3:9)?
3. Who are the ones pouring out these seven bowls on the earth? Who are the bowls being poured out on?
4. What are the signs, mentioned in Revelation 16:14, designed to do (1 Kings 22:20–23; Mark 13:22; Revelation 19:20)?
5. What will God's final act of judgment be on the earth before Christ's return?
6. What did the Holy Spirit highlight to you in Revelation 16 through the reading or the teaching?

Lesson 17: Revelation 17

I AM: The Women and the Scarlet Beast

Teaching Notes

Intro

Chapter 17 began with the image of a woman sitting on a scarlet beast. There were seven years of tribulation. In those seven years, there were seven seals, seven trumpets, seven bowls of God's wrath. Even in the middle of all of that, God still wanted the people to repent. At this point in the revelation, the battle of Armageddon has not happened yet. The book of Revelation is not always in chronological order. Christ has not come back yet at this point.

Teaching

Revelation 17:1–18: One of the seven angels who had one of the seven bowls had a conversation with John. Revelation 17 was about a Babylonian system—both the religious perspective of the harlot system and the Babylonian system that would include the Antichrist and Satan. Chapter 18 will cover Babylon's economic and political systems. In chapter 19, Christ comes and cleans everything up.

This chapter describes how the Babylonian system was not in step with how the city of God is conducted. There was always tension between the Babylonians and God. The image the angel showed John was the system of the prostitute who sat over the many waters.

Verse 2 states the kings of the world had committed sexual immorality with the prostitute. The kings of the earth were participating with the harlot's invitation. MacArthur explains, "The harlot will ally herself with the world's political leaders. Fornication here does not refer to sexual sin, but to idolatry. All the world rulers will be absorbed into the empire of Satan's false Christ."[1]

In the vision, the angel took John from an island and, in the Spirit, to a desert (v. 3). John saw a woman sitting on a scarlet beast that was covered with blasphemous names and that had seven heads and ten horns. This woman was known both as a harlot and as Babylon. Babylon was symbolic of a system against God, a system that was run by the Antichrist.

---

[1] John MacArthur, *The MacArthur Bible Commentary* (Nashville: Thomas Nelson, 2005), 2026.

Next, John described the appearance of the woman who wore purple and scarlet. She wore gold, precious stones, and pearls. She had a gold cup in her hand that was filled with everything vile. She assumed she was in control and was engaging herself with the nations and the leaders of the world. She became very wealthy in the process. The religious harlot was trying to lure people toward her.

Nelson's Commentary states, "The woman, Babylon, is dressed like a queen (18:7), wearing purple, scarlet, gold and pearls. Though the appearance of 'the great harlot' (vv. 1, 5) is regal, her royal golden cup is full of abominations . . . and filthiness, speaking of idolatry and unclean acts that disgust God."[2] This was an opposite picture of the Garden in Genesis. There was a cryptic name on her forehead, Babylon the Great, the mother of prostitutes and of the vile things of the earth. MacArthur explains, "It was customary for Roman prostitutes to wear a headband with their name on it (cf. Jeremiah 3:3), parading their wretchedness for all to see."[3] The golden cup was used to lead the nations into spiritual fornication. The goal was to get the nations to follow her. This Babylon the Great was distinctive from the geographical, historical city of Babylon.

From the Tower of Babel in Genesis 11 to Revelation 14:8, there were Babylons and representations of Babylons. The point of the Tower of Babel was for the people to make themselves equal to God. Everything else in Scripture extends from that picture of the Tower of Babel.

What we see at the end was the mother of all harlots in the cities and at the center of the power of all the systems. There was a domino effect as these cities fell over time. John's account was the end of these systems.

In verse 6, the system was assumed to be a success because they had killed those who followed Christ. MacArthur explains the phrase "the blood of the saints . . . martyrs of Jesus": "Some see the first group as Old Testament saints, and the second as New Testament saints—an unimportant distinction since this pictures the martyrs of the Tribulation."[4]

Constable had a perspective that "this system had destroyed true believers and rejoiced in their deaths. This revelation amazed John ('I wondered greatly'). A system purporting to honor God was killing His faithful followers!"[5]

In verse 7, the angel explained the secret meaning of the image of the beast and the seven heads and ten horns. Verse 8 identifies the Beast as the Antichrist,

---

[2] Earl D. Radmacher, Ronald B. Allen, and H. Wayne House, eds., *Nelson's New Illustrated Bible Commentary* (Nashville: Thomas Nelson, 1999), 1758.

[3] MacArthur, 2027.

[4] MacArthur, 2027.

[5] Thomas L. Constable, *Expository Notes of Dr. Thomas Constable: Revelation*, 284, https://planobiblechapel.org/tcon/notes/pdf/revelation.pdf.

and the system was the woman who sat on the Antichrist. The system was poured on, poured in, and poured through the Antichrist. The woman was against Christ.

The Antichrist was one who was, is, and will come again. The Antichrist would have a false resurrection. At the middle of the Great Tribulation, it seems the Antichrist will die and appear to come back to life. Those who do not have faith in Christ will be astonished. In Revelation 13:3–4 one of the heads for the Antichrist had a fatal wound from a sword, but it was healed. In Revelation 13:12–13, the false prophet encouraged people to worship the Antichrist because he had not died.

In verse 9 the seven heads are described as seven mountains. The woman was seated on the mountains. There were seven kings, and five had already fallen. There are numerous theories about the seven mountains. One theory is that the seven mountains represent the seven hills on which Rome was built. Another theory is that there were seven kingdoms and their kings. Out of the seven kings they may have represented: Egypt, Assyria, Babylon, Medo-Persia, Greece, Rome, and the last would be the Antichrist. John made a case that these systems were not of the Lord.

The Antichrist represents kingdoms seven and eight because of his death and resurrection. In verse 12, the ten horns represent the kingdoms under the Antichrist. They had authority from the Antichrist for just a period of time. The one hour that was referenced could represent three years during which they gave their power and authority to the Beast. These ten make war against the Lord of Lords and King of Kings. Verse 14 is about the Battle of Armageddon.

Verse 15 states the woman had authority over the people, the multitudes, the nations, and the languages. There would be one world religious system. Eventually, the Beast and all of the ten nations would hate the system. They would burn up the woman in fire. The Beast and the ten nations would be doing the Lord's will. Satan's own kingdom was divided against itself.

Closing

A kingdom divided against itself cannot stand. Mark 3:23–26 talked about the division of a kingdom in its own camp.

The Daily Word

As John's vision continues, preparation takes place for the battle that will occur when Christ's return begins. The kings of the earth, who had been given authority for one hour, give their power and authority to the beast. The kings join the beast and together wage war against the Lamb. But the Lamb of God, Jesus, *has victory* because He is the Lord of lords and the Kings of kings. His followers, the believers, fight with Him. He calls them chosen and faithful.

Jesus, the Savior of the earth, *reigns victorious* over all kingdoms—neither beast, nor king of the earth will gain victory over Him. He brings purpose, sovereignty, and works all things together for His good, for those He has *called chosen and who are faithful*. Do not fear when you face a battle, hardship, or unknown moments in life. As His called, faithful, and chosen, when you dwell in the shadow of the Almighty, you can say to the Lord: "My refuge and my fortress, my God, in whom I trust." Call to Him, and He will answer you. He will rescue you, satisfy you, and give you salvation. Today, do not fear, and do not be dismayed. The Lord promises hope in Him. He is your shelter. Take a deep breath and rest in the shadow of His mighty wings. He will be with you always.

These will make war against the Lamb, but the Lamb will conquer them because He is Lord of lords and King of kings. Those with Him are called, chosen, and faithful. —Revelation 17:14

Further Scripture: Psalm 91:1–2; John 15:16; James 2:5

Questions

1. What do you notice that God will show John about the great harlot in Revelation 17:1? What does John want us to know about her (Revelation 18:10, 18, 21)?

2. Who is the great harlot (Revelation 17:18)? Who will the great harlot align herself with in Revelation 17:2?

3. Compare Genesis 2 with Revelation 17:2–6. Notice the devastation that sin causes the world.

4. When will the ten horns receive authority (Revelation 17:12)? What is their one purpose, and who will they make war against?

5. Who will hate the harlot (Revelation 17:16)? Whose plan was it? How long will they have the kingdom (Genesis 50:20; Proverbs 19:21)?

6. What did the Holy Spirit highlight to you in Revelation 17 through the reading or the teaching?

Lesson 18: Revelation 18

I AM: The Fall of Babylon the Great

Teaching Notes

Intro

Revelation 1:4 gives the theme of the entire book of Revelation: "John: To the seven churches in Asia. Grace and peace to you from the One who is, who was, and who is coming; from the seven spirits before His throne." Chapters 1—3 document who Jesus is and was, and Chapters 4—5 proclaim how Jesus will return in the future. We are still covering the imagery of Revelation 1:4 today. In Revelation 16, we looked at the seven trumpets and then the four living creatures who handed seven bowls of wrath to seven angels. These seven wraths include for those who are not believers: (1) sores that will never go away; (2) seas of blood; (3) blood-contaminated drinking water; (4) sunburn from intense, ever-present heat; (5) darkness that comes over the Antichrist and his people; (6) the Euphrates River (1800 miles long) will dry up; and (7) enormous hail, each weighing 100 pounds, will fall on the cities. This is the wrath of God. Satan's wrath is possibly portrayed in the seven seals in Revelation.

In Revelation 17, the fall of Babylon and its religious system and the battle with Satan is outlined. Satan will eventually wage war against Jesus, the Lamb of God in the battle at Armageddon. Revelation 18 presents the commercial or economical side and the political side of the fall of Babylon. Revelation 19 outlines Jesus' return. The reason we have reviewed the bowls of wrath is because, at this point, the people were still in darkness (wrath #5).

Teaching

Revelation 18:1–3: John saw another angel with great authority descending from heaven, and the entire earth was illuminated by his splendor (v. 1). Even while the wrath of God continued, people were allowed to witness the glory of God. Constable summarizes verses 1–3 as "the first angelic announcement of judgment."[1] Wiersbe summarizes these same verses as "a voice of condemna-

---

[1] Thomas L. Constable, *Expository Notes of Dr. Thomas Constable: Revelation*, 295, https://planobiblechapel.org/tcon/notes/pdf/revelation.pdf.

tion."[2] Webster's Dictionary defines "condemnation" as "the act of condemning or pronouncing to be wrong; censure; blame." The angel will come down in God's glory to pronounce His displeasure with Babylon. The angel proclaimed that the Babylonian system had failed, becoming a dwelling place for demons, unclean spirits, and even unclean birds and animals (v. 2). The system was so corrupt the demonic dwelled there instead of in the great abyss. The reality is the demonic are present today (Ephesians 6:12). Why do we not address this today? There are times when the angelic beings are fighting demonic forces for us. Not only was Babylon guilty, other nations had been drawn into the Babylonian's system. The kings were drawn into sexual immorality, and the merchants became wealthy with excessive greed (v. 3).

Revelation 18:4–8: Wiersbe summarizes verses 4–8 as, "The voice of separation."[3] Another voice from heaven called for believers to get out of Babylon so they would not get caught up in its sin and its plagues (v. 4). MacArthur points out, "God will call His own to disentangle themselves from this evil system. This may also be God's calling the elect to abandon the world system and come to faith in the Savior."[4] The voice explained that Babylon's sins were so great they were piled up to heaven and God was focused on those sins (v. 5). Wiersbe points out, "John offered two reasons for God's people separating themselves from the diabolical system. The first is that they might avoid pollution, becoming 'partakers of her sins' (1 Timothy 5:22; Revelation 18:4)."[5] "The second reason is that God's people might be spared the terrible plagues He will send on Babylon."[6]

In verse 6, John heard a voice say the woman should be paid back double according to her sins (Isaiah 51:19–22). MacArthur explains, "The angel calls for God to recompense wrath to Babylon in her own cup to repay her according to her deeds. This is an echo of the Old Testament law of retaliation, which will be implemented by God."[7] Double the judgment was coming. The widow had glorified herself and saw herself as a queen (v. 7). She was deserving of the judgment to come. Therefore, the plagues she would face would come in one day at one time—death, grief, and famine (v. 8).

---

[2] Warren W. Wiersbe, *The Bible Exposition Commentary: Ephesians–Revelation* (Colorado Springs: David C. Cook, 1989), 614.

[3] Wiersbe, 614.

[4] John MacArthur, *The MacArthur Bible Commentary* (Nashville: Thomas Nelson, 2005), 2029.

[5] Wiersbe, 614.

[6] Wiersbe, 615.

[7] MacArthur, 2029.

Revelation 18:9–19: Wiersbe summarized these verses as "the voice of lamentation."[8] Not only would the woman be burned up, but the earthly kings who had supported her and participated in her religious and economic systems would not survive either (v. 9). Babylon will fall in one day (Daniel 5:30–31). MacArthur points out that the word for mourn or lament comes from the same Greek word that means "to express the despair of the unbelieving world at the return of Christ."[9] The kings will lament because they cannot get what they want—everything they had or want will be gone. In fear, the kings will stand as far away from the woman's judgment as possible (v. 10).

The merchants will also mourn because no one will buy what they sell (vv. 11–13). The merchants will lose their businesses. MacArthur suggests, "The slave trade, long banned by the civilized nations of the world, will reappear in Antichrist's debauched commercial system."[10] The things they desired and had value to them will leave them and will never be available to them again (v. 14). The merchants will stand by in fear and mourning that everything will be wiped out in an hour (vv. 15–17a).

The shipmasters, seafarers, and the sailors also watch selfishly, mourning from afar that they would no longer make a living by the sea (vv. 17a–19). The question in verse 18 really proclaims their loss of hope. If Babylon can fall, then no other equal options were available to them. Where do you turn when everything you know and value is lost? The sea people could only see Babylon as their answer. In hopelessness, they threw dust on their heads and kept mourning their loss. If only they had been willing to cry out to the Lord in their hopelessness (Joshua 7:6; 1 Samuel 4:12; Job 2:12).

Revelation 18:20–24: Wiersbe summarizes these final verses as "the voice of celebration."[11] In verse 20, the people of God were told to rejoice and celebrate because He has executed judgment on Babylon. God avenged all the works of Satan and the Antichrist against His people. Then, a mighty angel threw a large millstone into the sea to show how Babylon would be thrown down and destroyed (v. 21). The people of Babylon will never celebrate, never work, never trade again (v. 22). No life in Babylon will continue—no marriages, no light for them will ever be seen again (v. 23).

---

[8] Wiersbe, 615.

[9] MacArthur, 2029.

[10] MacArthur, 2030.

[11] Wiersbe, 616.

Closing

Constable points out that the angel gave three reasons for why Babylon would face such devastation: "First, men whom the world regards as great have enriched themselves and lifted themselves up in pride because of Babylon's influence (cf. Isaiah 23:8). Second, as a result of the first reason, Babylon has seduced all nations."[12] Third, Babylon slew God's saints.[13]

The Daily Word

John's vision continued as the great city of Babylon fell to destruction forever. The political leaders fell, the merchants fell, and all who did business by the sea fell. All were destroyed. God wiped away everything they had built up with their hands and had placed their hope in. It affected other kingdoms, and the people wept and lamented. Pride and seduction filled Babylon. Now, at last, *they received this final judgment.*

Whom and what do you put your hope in? If the stock market crashed, if your car was destroyed, if you were laid off from your executive position, or if you were unable to exercise daily, would it cause you to crumble and lament? Or would you remain strong in the Lord because your hope rests in Him? When life falls apart, your response will honestly reveal what or whom you have placed your hope in. Choose to rest in the Lord's promise to work all things together for good. He has a plan, and He has control over all the earth. He will carry your burdens. Choose to not only believe His truth but live out your belief that *God is bigger than the temporary pleasures this life offers.* May your life reflect His faithfulness as you put your hope in Him.

He cried in a mighty voice:
It has fallen,
Babylon the Great has fallen!
She has become a dwelling for demons,
a haunt for every unclean spirit,
a haunt for every unclean bird,
and a haunt for every unclean and despicable beast. —Revelation 18:2

Further Scripture: 2 Corinthians 4:16–18; Revelation 18:16–17a, 23b–24

---

[12] Constable, 305.

[13] Constable, 305.

Questions

1. In Revelation 18:2, what do you think it means when it says fallen Babylon has "become a dwelling place of demons and a prison of every unclean spirit, and a prison of every unclean and hateful bird" (Isaiah 13:21)?

2. When you read Revelation 18:4, do you think of Sodom? Where else in Scripture are God's people warned to separate from a place or people (Genesis 19:12–13, 17; Isaiah 48:20; 52:11; Jeremiah 51:6, 45; 2 Corinthians 6:17)?

3. Where in Scripture do we first hear about Babylon (Babel)? Read Genesis 11:4. What were the people's aspirations? Read Revelation 18:5. How do these two verses relate?

4. Revelation 18:7 and Isaiah 47:7–8 note that Babylon called herself a queen and not a widow. In fact, twice in Isaiah 47, Babylon is quoted to have said in her heart, "I am, and there is no one besides me" (Isaiah 47:8, 10). Note the almost exact wording of the Lord in Isaiah 46:9. Why do you think she (Babylon) is described as being clothed in fine linen, purple, and scarlet, and adorned with gold and precious stones and pearls (Exodus 39; 40; Revelation 17:4a; 18:16; 21:18–21)?

5. Do you think there are deliberate contrasts between the fall of Babylon the Great and the new heaven and earth (weeping or mourning: Revelation 18:15, 19; 21:4; lamp or light: Revelation 18:23a; 21:23; kings of the earth: Revelation 18:3; 21:24; the nation's interaction: Revelation 18:3; 21:25–26; unholy vs. holy: Revelation 18:2–3; 21:27)? Can you find others not listed here?

6. Revelation 18:22 specifically records that no musicians or instruments will be heard any longer in Babylon. Do you think this is a connection to Daniel 3:5, 7, and 15? Note that the consequence for not worshipping the image in Daniel 3:15 was to be cast into a furnace of blazing fire. Read Revelation 18:8 and 18. Do you think Babylon's destruction is divine justice?

7. What did the Holy Spirit highlight to you in Revelation 18 through the reading or the teaching?

Lesson 19: Revelation 19

I AM: Feasts of Judgments

Teaching Notes

Intro

Revelation 19 is a famous and often-studied chapter in Revelation. This chapter contains the picture of Jesus returning on a white horse and of the Battle of Armageddon. All of the seals, the trumpets, and the bowls, everything we have dealt with about the Antichrist and Babylon, has led to this chapter. Revelation 19 serves as a bridge from the Great Tribulation to the Millennial Kingdom—from the seven years of tribulation to the 1,000-year reign of Jesus.

Teaching

Revelation 19:1–6: "After this" refers to the fall of Babylon (v. 1). The city's fall prompted a vast multitude in heaven to speak for the first of four times in this chapter. Who makes up the vast multitude (v. 1)? They could be the saints from Revelation 7, angels, or a mixture of both. MacArthur highlighted five reasons for this praise: "(1) God's deliverance of His people from their enemies (v. 1); (2) God's judgement are out of justice (v. 2); (3) God's permanent crushing of man's rebellion (v. 3); (4) God's sovereignty (v. 6); and (5) God's communion with His people (v. 7)."[1]

The 24 elders in verse 4 could be a representation of the church, of Israel, or of the 12 apostles and the 12 tribes. The "four living creatures" are the lion, the calf, the eagle, and the animal with a man's face.

Revelation 19:7–10: The multitude praised God because, at this time, He will usher in His kingdom. A new government will exist, and Jesus will reign. *Nelson's Commentary* points out that this government is "not a democracy, but a theocracy—a government by God when the 'Lord God Omnipotent' shall reign in righteousness (Isaiah 11)."[2]

---

[1] John MacArthur, *The MacArthur Bible Commentary* (Nashville: Thomas Nelson, 2005), 2030.

[2] Earl D. Radmacher, Ronald B. Allen, and H. Wayne House, eds., *Nelson's New Illustrated Bible Commentary* (Nashville: Thomas Nelson, 1999), 1761.

The multitude praised God "because the marriage of the Lamb has come, and His wife has prepared herself" (v. 7). In the Old Testament, Israel is described as God's wife. In the New Testament, the church is described as Christ's bride. Ephesians 5:23 and 32 explain: "For the husband is the head of the wife as Christ is the head of the church. He is the Savior of the body. . . . This mystery is profound, but I am talking about Christ and the church." In verse 7, Jesus is referred to as "The Lamb."

2 Corinthian 7:1 says: "Therefore, dear friends, since we have such promises, let us cleanse ourselves from every impurity of the flesh and spirit, completing our sanctification in the fear of God." Perhaps one of the reasons Christ has not yet returned is that His bride, the church, has not prepared herself. Jude 21 says, "Keep yourselves in the love of God, expecting the mercy of our Lord Jesus Christ for eternal life." MacArthur notes the marriage feast described in verse 10 will represent the completion of the marriage ceremony where we will celebrate the five reasons the multitude praised God throughout this chapter.[3]

A blessing was pronounced on everyone invited to the marriage feast of the Lamb (v. 9). But if Jesus is the groom and the church is the bride, who will be invited to the feast? Some other group is obviously described here, but who are they? They could be the Old Testament saints, those saved by grace through faith before Pentecost who will also reign with Christ during the millennial kingdom, or they could be the tribulation saints.[4]

After seeing this, John "fell at his feet to worship" the angel who showed him these things. The angel stopped John and exhorted him to "worship God, because the testimony about Jesus is the spirit of prophecy" (v. 10). Jesus was the theme of Old Testament prophecy. He was the cord that held it all together.

Revelation 19:11–16: John saw Jesus, who was referred to as "Faithful and True," riding on a white horse. Now, Jesus "judges and makes war in righteousness" (v. 11). In this depiction, Jesus "had a name written that no one knows except Himself" (v. 12) similarly to Revelation 3:12: "The victor: I will make him a pillar in the sanctuary of My God, and he will never go out again. I will write on him the name of My God and the name of the city of My God—the new Jerusalem, which comes down out of heaven from My God—and My new name." His robe is bloodstained, and "His name is the Word of God"(v. 13). The blood on His robe is not blood from the battle of Armageddon. *Nelson's Commentary* suggests the blood could be from His redemptive death, the trampling of the winepress of God's wrath, or both.[5]

---

[3] MacArthur, 2031.

[4] MacArthur, 2031.

[5] Radmacher et al., 1762.

"The armies that were in heaven" who followed Jesus (v. 14) could be the church, Old Testament believers, tribulation saints, or angels.[6] MacArthur observed that the armies of heaven "return not to help Jesus in the battle (they are unarmed), but to reign with him after He defeats His enemies."[7] The sharp sword that comes out of His mouth depicts the power Jesus will have to kill His enemies.

Revelation 19:17–21: The battle of Armageddon happens here. It begins with an angel calling to the birds to gather "for the great supper of God" (v. 17). This is not the marriage feast of the Lamb that was described earlier in Revelation 19. Instead, it is the coming of God's final judgment that will see the birds "eat the flesh of kings, the flesh of commanders, the flesh of mighty men, the flesh of horses and of their riders, and the flesh of everyone, both free and slave, small and great" (v. 18).

In verse 19, the beast is the Antichrist and the kings of the earth are the ten nations. They gather together to fight against Jesus and His army. During the battle, the beast and the false prophet will be taken prisoner and will be "thrown alive into the lake of fire that burns with sulfur" (v. 20). Revelation 20:10 states: "The Devil who deceived them was thrown into the lake of fire and sulfur where the beast and the prophet are, and they will be tormented day and night forever." Daniel 7:11 prophesized: "I watched, then, because of the sound of the arrogant words the horn was speaking. As I continued watching, the beast was killed and its body destroyed and given over to the burning fire."

Eternal punishment awaits Satan, the beast, and the prophet. The beast's armies "were killed with the sword that came from the mouth of the rider of the horse" (v. 21).

Closing

Jesus will reign in victory and defeat all who stand against Him and the armies of heaven get to join Him. He does all of the fighting on behalf of His people.

The Daily Word

After the complete destruction of Babylon, a vast multitude of voices sang hallelujah and praises to the Lord for His deliverance, judgment, and sovereignty. Then, in John's vision, *heaven opened and a rider called Faithful and True, the Word of God—yes, Jesus—came out riding on a white horse.* His army of believers followed Him, and He fought the battle against the beast and the false prophet.

---

[6] MacArthur, 2032.

[7] MacArthur, 1023.

When captured, the beast and false prophet were thrown alive into the lake of fire that burns with sulfur. With a sword in His mouth, Jesus killed the beast's entire army.

Allow Jesus' victory over the beast, the false prophet, and their army serve as an encouragement to you today as you *fight your own battles*, not against flesh and blood, but against the rulers, authorities, world powers of darkness, and spiritual forces of evil in the heavens. *You have victory in the Great I Am*—Jesus Christ—who is coming back to defeat the enemy. But until then, hold up the sword of the spirit and shield of faith. Walk with the breastplate of righteousness and the helmet of salvation. Steadily go with the feet of peace and with truth like a belt around your waist. Stand firm. Be alert. Pray at all times. *The enemy will flee when you boldly say the name of Jesus!* Hallelujah! Say it again. Hallelujah! Salvation, glory, and power belong to our God!

But the beast was taken prisoner, and along with him the false prophet, who had performed the signs in his presence. He deceived those who accepted the mark of the beast and those who worshiped his image with these signs. Both of them were thrown alive into the lake of fire that burns with sulfur. —Revelation 19:20

Further Scripture: 1 Corinthians 15:57; Ephesians 6:14–18; Revelation 19:1, 11–13

Questions

1. The 24 elders were mentioned in several other places in Revelation (Revelation 4:4; 5:8; 11:16; 19:4). Who do you think the 24 elders might be? What Scripture did you use to back your answer up?

2. The sound of many waters was mentioned (Revelation 19:6). Where else in Scripture was the sound of many waters mentioned (Ezekiel 1:24; 43:2; Revelation 1:15; 14:2)?

3. In Revelation 19:15, was the sword mentioned the same type of sword that was mentioned in Hebrews 4:12 (Revelation 1:16; 2:12)? Why do you think that?

4. Read Ezekiel 39:18–20. How does it compare to Revelation 19:17–18? Do both refer to the same event? Did the Lord make the point that kings will be no better and end up the same as the slaves, being eaten by the birds? Why or why not?

5. What did the Holy Spirit highlight to you in Revelation 19 through the reading or the teaching?

Lesson 20: Revelation 20

I AM: The Millennial Reign of Christ

Teaching Notes

Intro

Revelation 19 records that Jesus is coming back on a white horse to clean house. The nations will be destroyed, and the beast and the false prophet will be thrown into a lake of fire. Everything we have been reading since the Garden of Eden is coming to a head (Genesis 3). The word we have used for the book of Genesis was *SEED*, and the word we have used for the book of Revelation is *I AM*. From the beginning of time until today, Christ was and is present. The battle of Armageddon has already happened as we start chapter 20. Chapter 20 starts to show the process of restoration.

Teaching

Revelation 20:1–2: The angel with the key to the abyss seized Satan and bound him for 1,000 years. The angel was also carrying a chain. You have to believe there was some kind of struggle here, that Satan did not go willingly into chains for 1,000 years. This would have happened after the battle of Armageddon, and Jesus would have already been on earth. There is a great theological debate here. People love to discuss whether Satan was really bound for 1,000 years or if it was symbolic. I believe he was bound for 1,000 years.

Revelation 20:3: Remember that the beast (the Antichrist) and the false prophet were already in the abyss or lake of fire. Now, Satan would join them. People call this time the Millennium. MacArthur outlines the three major schools of thoughts on this 1,000 years bondage.

1. "Premillennialism interprets this as a literal 1,000 year period during which Jesus Christ, in fulfilment of numerous Old Testament prophecies (2 Samuel 7:12–16; Psalm 2; Isaiah 11:6–12; 24:23; Hosea 3:4, 5; Joel 3:9–21; Amos 9:8–15; Micah 4:1–8; Zephaniah 3:14–20; Zechariah 14:1–11; Matthew 24:29–31, 36–44), reigns on the earth."

2. "Postmillennialism understands the reference to a 1,000-year period as only symbolic of a golden age of righteousness and spiritual prosperity. It will be ushered in by the spread of the gospel during the present church age and brought to completion when Christ returns. According to this view, references to Christ's reign on earth primarily describes His spiritual reign in the hearts of believers in the church."

3. "Amillennialism understands the 1,000 years to be merely symbolic of a long period of time. This view interprets Old Testament prophecies of a Millennium as being fulfilled spiritually now in the church (either on earth or in heaven) or as references to the eternal state."[1]

I have never really taken a stance, but it is hard not to when you see what is to come. John wrote that ultimately Satan is going to be released and then imprisoned again. I think if you do not take the 1,000 years literally, it makes it very hard to interpret Revelation 20—22. We are going to use the argument that it points to a literal 1,000 years. After those years, Satan is going to be released. MacArthur states, "Satan will be released so God can make a permanent end of sin before establishing a new heaven and earth."[2] Satan will make a final stand with those that reject Christ, and they will be crushed.

Revelation 20:4: Those who were martyred for rejecting the mark of the beast will rise up and rule with Christ, having been given the authority to judge for these 1,000 years. John saw a bodily resurrection. Tom Constable outlines times God has resurrected or will resurrect or raise the righteous:

- "First, He raised Jesus Christ who is the first fruits of those who sleep (1 Corinthians 15:23)."
- "Second, He raised some saints near Jerusalem shortly after Jesus' resurrection (Matthew 27:52–53)."
- "Third, He will raise Christians at the Rapture (1 Thessalonians 4:13–18)."
- "Fourth, He will raise the two witnesses during the Great Tribulation (Revelation 11:3, 11)."
- "Fifth, He will raise the Tribulation martyrs at the beginning of the Millennium (Revelation 20:4–5)."
- "Sixth, He will raise the Old Testament saints at the same time (Isaiah 26:19–21; Ezekiel 37:12–14; Daniel 12:2–4)."

---

[1] John MacArthur, *The MacArthur Bible Commentary* (Nashville: Thomas Nelson, 2005), 2034.

[2] MacArthur, 2034.

- "Seventh, He will apparently raise the saints who die during the Millennium . . . (Revelation 20:12–13)."[3]

This seems to be a pattern of the Lord. He has no problem bringing people back to life. In this context, we see the tribulation martyrs coming back to life. We have to interpret these verses with consistency, so if you say the 1,000 years are symbolic, what are you going to do with verse 4?

Revelation 20:5: Many scholars suggest those resurrected after the 1,000-year period would be the bodies of the unbelievers. These unbelievers have not yet been judged.

Revelation 20:6: The first resurrection is the resurrection of life. MacArthur writes the resurrection of life is "'the resurrection of the just' (Luke 14:14), the resurrection of 'those who are Christ's at His coming' (1 Corinthians 15:23), and the 'better resurrection' (Hebrews 11:35). It includes only the redeemed church age, the Old Testament, and Tribulation. They will enter the kingdom in resurrection bodies, along with believers who survived the Tribulation."[4] Believers will reign and rule with Christ for these 1,000 years. The second death has no power over them. "The first death is only physical; the second is spiritual and eternal in the lake of fire, the final, eternal hell."[5] There are seven "blessed" statements in Revelation. Here John wrote, "Blessed and holy is the one who shares in the first resurrection!" Those who die in the Lord are blessed with the privilege of entering His kingdom.

Revelation 20:7: After the 1,000 years, Christ is still king on earth. Christ has all His believers with Him, but there will still be nonbelievers. That 1,000 years is not a period of glorification here on earth. There will still be sin. Satan will be released in order to have one last shot. We know he will fail.

Revelation 20:8–9: Technically there are two battles—the battle of Armageddon and the battle after Satan is released. Satan will gather a huge army that surrounds the "encampment of the saints." A fire will come down from heaven and consume them (all of the enemy).

---

[3] Thomas L. Constable, *Expository Notes of Dr. Thomas Constable: Revelation*, 337, https://planobiblechapel.org/tcon/notes/pdf/revelation.pdf.

[4] MacArthur, 2035.

[5] MacArthur, 2035.

Revelation 20:10: Again, remember that, at this point, the beast and the false prophet are still in the lake of fire. The devil will now join them and will be tortured day and night forever. There have been incredible teachers of the Bible who have gone astray, saying hell does not exist. If that's true, why did Jesus die on the cross? He was resurrected from the cross in order to give us life. He also didn't want us to experience this torture day and night forever. When you take away "the tormenting day and night," you take away the power of the cross. People want to make the message soft.

Revelation 20:11–15: This will be the final judgment of Satan. It will be done and officially over. Now we begin to see the great white throne of judgment. The unbelievers who were raised after the 1000 year period are to be judged by their actions and thoughts on earth. Those who reject Christ will all face judgment. No one is exempt. No longer does death have a place.

Closing

Some say not to preach hell when trying to convert someone to Christ. I say, do it! Jesus has so much to offer. Hell is real. Revelation should drive us to truth, love, and compassion. If your name is not written in the Book of Life, you're not getting in. No one should have to face that. I hope we can use this as a motivation to share Christ. Judgment is around the corner.

The Daily Word

After the devil was defeated and thrown into the lake of fire and sulfur to be tormented day and night, forever and ever, John saw the One, *Jesus, seated on the great white throne with the books opened.* The final judgment came, separating those who believe in Jesus and those who never repented and received Jesus as Savior. It was judgment time. *Anyone whose name was not written in the Book of Life was thrown into the lake of fire* to be tormented day and night, forever and ever, along with Satan, the antichrist, and the false prophet.

As you witness the victory Jesus has over Satan, you also witness the hard reality for the unsaved. As the Word of God states, those who have not confessed Jesus as Lord and Savior, whose names are not written in the Book of Life, will be thrown into the lake of fire. May John's vision of what is to come in the end prepare you to be ready. Today, seek the Lord as your Savior and eternal hope for salvation. May it stir compassion within you to share Christ's love with others. May it motivate you to pray and beseech the Lord to save people you know and love while there is still time. You wouldn't want someone you love to ask at the end, *"Why didn't anyone ever share this Jesus with me?"* Go now and share the gospel. *What are you waiting for?*

And anyone not found written in the book of life was thrown into the lake of fire. —Revelation 20:15

Further Scripture: Psalm 33:4–5; Philippians 4:3; Revelation 20:10

Questions

1. Is the bottomless pit mentioned in Revelation 20:1 the same as the pit in Revelation 9:1? Why or why not?
2. Take a few minutes and try to imagine a world without Satan and his evil ones being among us during those 1,000 years he is locked up. What do you see it being like?
3. Revelation 20:4–6 speaks about the dead being risen. What is the second death and why does it have no power over those who were raised to life to reign with Christ (Revelation 2:11; 20:14; 21:8)?
4. Do you find thoughts about the great white throne judgment intimidating or scary in Revelation 20:11–15? How can you be sure that your name is in the Lamb's Book of Life (Romans 10:9–10)? Do you know someone with whom you can share the saving knowledge of Christ? Share with them so they can know that their name is in the same Book of Life.
5. What did the Holy Spirit highlight to you in Revelation 20 through the reading or the teaching?

Lesson 21: Revelation 21

I AM: The New Jerusalem

Teaching Notes

Intro

We have two days to finish up the book of Revelation and to finish up all 66 books of the Bible. reviveSCHOOL has become so much more than we ever expected! One of the things we didn't think about was how the Word would impact us! Our team had grown so much. We are going to be talking about a new heaven and a new earth, and it makes sense. No, I can't picture everything. But when you go back and start studying in Genesis, it all builds to these final chapters. It feels right. At the end of chapter 20, everyone who doesn't know Christ was thrown into the lake of fire. Everyone includes Satan, the beast, and the false prophet, who will all be tortured night and day forever.

Teaching

Revelation 21:1–2: John saw a vision of a new start. There will be a new heaven and a new earth. There will no sea, no water. Praise God, because anytime I think of water used in Revelation, it is always used in judgment and torture. This new heaven and new earth are the fulfillment of Old Testament and New Testament prophecy (Psalm 102:25–26; Isaiah 65:17; 66:22; Luke 21:33; Hebrews 1:10–12). I want to show you that this is not a new revelation. John presents us with a unique picture of the New Jerusalem, which has already been established. It is literally coming down from heaven, the capital city and the perfect place of holiness. MacArthur wrote, "It is seen 'coming down out of heaven' indicating it already existed; but it descends into the new heavens and new earth from its place on high. This is the city where the saints will live (John 14:1–3)."[1] When I look at this picture, it becomes surreal.

Revelation 21:3–5: Christ coming to earth to die on the cross is a foreshadowing of the new heaven and new earth. Revelation 7:15 is the fulfillment of verse three. We are going to be invited to see the heavenly throne. Psalm 132 references

---

[1] John MacArthur, *The MacArthur Bible Commentary* (Nashville: Thomas Nelson, 2005), 2036.

God's dwelling place over and over. This imagery happens after the 1,000 year millennium. This is the picture of heaven we talk about—no more grief, pain, or tears (Isaiah 25:8; 1 Corinthians 15:54–58; 2 Corinthians 5:17). This becomes a complete fulfillment of the Word of God. To me, this is a picture of the comparison from Genesis to Revelation. Tom Constable gave us the following chart to look at.[2]

Genesis		Revelation	
Heavens and earth created	(1:1)	New heavens and earth	(21:1)
Sun created	(1:16)	No need of the sun	(21:23)
The night established	(1:5)	No night there	(21:25; 22:5)
The seas created	(1:10)	No more seas	(21:1)
The curse announced	(3:14–17)	No more curse	(22:3)
Death enters history	(3:19)	No more death	(21:4)
Man driven from paradise	(3:24)	Man restored to paradise	(22:14)
Sorrow and pain begin	(3:17)	No more mourning, crying, or pain	(21:4)

I want us to be able to see the original creation and then how God restores it. It is a pretty powerful image. Verse 5 reminds us of Revelation 19:11, where we see Jesus coming back on a white horse and His words were faithful and true.

Revelation 21:6–8: It is done! What a picture! What is it that is done? It is the task of wrath. Jesus is in the beginning and the end. From Genesis to Revelation, Jesus is there. The water Jesus will give is the water of life. His water will never dry up; thus, there is no need for the sea. Those who overcome and those who believe in Christ are the victors (1 John 5:4–5). The victors will be the sons of God who have a spiritual inheritance. The unbelievers will find their inheritance in the lake of fire—the second death. The first death is the physical death, and the second death is for unbelievers who will spend their eternity in the lake of fire.

Verse 8 lists cowards, unbelievers, those who are vile, murderers, those who are sexually immoral, sorcerers, idolaters, and all liars. All of these lifestyles will send you to hell. I am pretty sure everyone has probably told a lie. At some point, many might deal with cowardice in regards to sexual immorality. The judgment is

---

[2] Thomas L. Constable, *Expository Notes of Dr. Thomas Constable: Revelation*, 352–53, https://planobiblechapel.org/tcon/notes/pdf/revelation.pdf.

on a lifestyle, not a sin. This serves as a warning to not give in to these toxic types of lifestyles. Paul even warns us against these things in 1 Corinthians 6:9–10.

The message is pretty clear—these lifestyles are unacceptable. The good part is when you put your trust in Christ, He will change all of that?

Revelation 21:9–14: In these verses, we begin to see characteristics of the new Jerusalem. MacArthur wrote, "The new Jerusalem takes on the character of its inhabitants, the redeemed" (Revelation 19:7–9, 21:2).[3] Constable explains, "Verses 11–22 [describe] physical features of the city."[4] The city had 12 high walls that are guarded by 12 angels. The gates are named after the sons of the 12 tribes of Israel (Ezekiel 48:30–35). We know there will be three gates on each side of the city—the south, east, north, and west. There will be 12 foundations that will have the name of the 12 apostles (Luke 6:13–16; Ephesians 2:20). Remember in Matthew 19:28, Jesus told the apostles that they would have a prominent place in heaven with Him.

Revelation 21:15–16: A gold rod (reed) was used to measure the city. MacArthur wrote, "The reed was about ten feet long, which was for a standard of measure."[5] The 12,000 stadia, or furlongs, is a symbol of perfection. MacArthur explains, "12,000 furlongs would be nearly 1,400 miles cubed or about two million square miles, offering plenty of room for all the glorified saints to live. . . . The city has the symmetrical dimensions of a perfect cube."[6] It's really big. The closet parallel on earth would be the inner sanctuary of the temple.

Revelation 21:17–21: The width of the wall measures 144 cubits, which is 73 yards or 216 feet. The wall is made of jasper. Jasper is probably like the material of a diamond. The city is made of pure gold. The gold will be clear so the radiance of God can reflect and shine. The foundations will have a precious stone adorned to it, probably having something to do with the apostles. There are 12 different, unique stones, eight of which were on the breastplate of the high priest. Each gate is made of a single pearl. The street is also made of transparent gold.

Revelation 21:22–27: There will be no sanctuary or temple because the Lord God the Almighty and the Lamb are the sanctuary. The glory of God will illuminate the heavens. The nations will walk in light and bring their glory and honor into it. The gates will never close and there will never be night. There is no more sin,

---

[3] MacArthur, 2037.

[4] Constable, 364.

[5] MacArthur, 2038.

[6] MacArthur, 2038.

there are no more unbelievers. The Jews and the Gentiles can come together before the throne. This is the same picture as Revelation 3:5.

Closing

Why would we stay quiet about this new heaven and this new earth? We have a chance every day to share the truth of the new heaven and the new earth. God has offered His love and redemption to all; He just asks us to share His words. We have one more chapter until we bring the canon of Scripture to a close. See you tomorrow.

The Daily Word

The marriage previously announced between the Bride and the Lamb finally occurs. John witnesses the holy New Jerusalem radiantly coming down out of heaven, ready for God like a bride meeting her husband. John sees the new heaven and new earth, where God will dwell with humanity. Death, grief, pain, and crying will no longer exist. The One seated on the throne instructs John to write these words because they are beautiful and true: "It Is done! I am the Alpha and the Omega, the Beginning and the End. I will give water as a gift to the thirsty from the spring of life. The *victor will inherit these things*, and I will be his God, and he will be My son."

Who is the victor to inherit these things? If you simply have faith to believe Jesus is the Son of God, then you can reign victorious in heaven forever with the Alpha and the Omega and drink from the spring of life forever. You will experience no more tears and no more pain, you will walk on golden streets in the light of God's glory, and your name will be written in the Lamb's Book of Life. *Jesus gave you the power and authority to share this good, life-changing message. Why stay quiet?* Today, go and share the beauty and hope inherited by the victors who have faith in Jesus.

"Write, because these words are faithful and true." And He said to me, "It is done! I am the Alpha and the Omega, the Beginning and the End. I will give water as a gift to the thirsty from the spring of life. The victor will inherit these things, and I will be his God, and he will be My son."
—Revelation 21:5b–7

Further Scripture: 1 John 5:4–5; Revelation 21:3–4, 9b–11

Questions

1. According to Revelation 21:1, why will there no longer be any sea in the new heaven and new earth?

2. In Revelation 21:3 John heard a voice saying, "God's dwelling is with humanity, and He will live with them." Yet, verse 22 tells us that there is no temple in the New Jerusalem. Explain why you think this is.

3. What do you think Revelation 21:4 means by "the previous things have passed away"? What are these "previous things"?

4. Why do you think there are high walls and 12 gates around the New Jerusalem (Revelation 21:12)? Why have gates if they'll never be closed (Revelation 21:25)?

5. Who are those who are able to enter into the New Jerusalem (Revelation 21:27)? Who cannot enter?

6. What did the Holy Spirit highlight to you in Revelation 21 through the reading or the teaching?

Lesson 22: Revelation 22

I AM: The Source of Life

Teaching Notes

Intro

It's hard to believe this is the last lesson of reviveSCHOOL. We have gone through 730 lessons. I'm feeling very emotional about this today. This team has worked so hard for two years as we have plowed through the Word of God together. Hebrews 4:12 says, "For the word of God is living and effective and sharper than any double-edged sword, penetrating as far as the separation of soul and spirit, joints and marrow. It is able to judge the ideas and thoughts of the heart." The Bible is so alive and active, and when we started reviveSCHOOL we wanted it to become active and alive in our work, in our churches, and in our people.

Jesus said, "Don't assume I came to destroy the Law or the Prophets. I did not come to destroy but to fulfill" (Matthew 5:17). Revelation 22 is all that fulfillment. Revelation and the coming of Christ is literally about overcoming sin and death. I feel like God told us at Time to Revive to slow down and spend time in His Word. I honestly never thought I would be changed so much in the process. The entire Bible is life-changing, and it's all about Christ. This two-year process has been the toughest time of ministry that I have had—being obedient enough to stay in the Word long enough to begin to see the bigger picture of the Messiah.

Teaching

Revelation 22:1–5: John was shown a river of living water flowing from the throne of God and the Lamb down the middle of the street (v. 1). MacArthur states, "This river is unlike any on earth because no hydrological cycle exists."[1] The idea of living water is seen throughout Scripture (Ezekiel 47; John 7:38–39). The tree of life was on both sides of the river, producing twelve kinds of fruit, producing fruit every month (v. 2). The tree of life is first presented in Genesis 3:22–24. No one has access to the tree of life until it's shown in Revelation 22. The leaves of the tree of life will be used for healing (restoring) the nations (Ezekiel 47:12).

---

[1] John MacArthur, *The MacArthur Bible Commentary* (Nashville: Thomas Nelson, 2005), 2039.

The throne of God and the Lamb will be in the city and His slaves (us, as His servants) will serve Him (v. 3). I am not sure what all this means except that we will be worshipping the Lord continually. His servants will see His face, and His name will be on their foreheads (v. 4). Our goal as believers is to see Him face-to-face (1 Corinthians 13:12). This is describing the new heaven and the new earth. There will be no night or darkness, because God will provide the light, and they will reign forever (v. 5). *Nelson's Commentary* points out that "no night . . . no lamp" fulfills Christ's proclamation of Himself as the "light of the world"[2] (John 8:12; 9:5; 12:46). This is a picture of paradise being restored.

Revelation 22:6–7: The angel said the words were "faithful and true" (v. 6), using the language of the "Faithful and True" Lord returning on a white horse (Revelation 19:11). The Lord will come quickly, so "the one who keeps the prophetic words of this book is blessed" (v. 7). The book of Revelation refers to being "blessed" seven times; this is the sixth. The blessings of God are found in the book of Revelation and in learning how to walk out the promises of God.

Revelation 22:8–11: John stated he was the one who heard and saw all these things, and when he did, he fell at the feet of the angel to worship (v. 8). This was the second time John mistakenly fell before the angel to worship him (Revelation 19:10). The angel reminded John that he was a fellow servant with him, the prophets, and those who keep the words of the book of Revelation. Only God is to be worshipped (v. 9). The angel also told John not to seal up the words of his vision because the time was near (v. 10). In Revelation 10:4, John was told to keep certain prophecies sealed up. MacArthur explains, "These prophesies are to be proclaimed so they can produce obedience and worship."[3] MacArthur also states, "Those who reject God's warnings will fix their eternal destiny in hell, where they will retain their evil and filthy natures for all eternity."[4] However, those who are righteous will remain righteous, and the holy will remain holy (v. 11).

Revelation 22:12–14: John was reminded that the Lord was coming quickly (v. 12a) (Revelation 3:11; 22:7). God will reward the works that each has done that survive His testing eternally (v. 12b) (1 Corinthians 9:24–27). We have experienced the discipline in reviveSCHOOL that caused our faith and maturity in the Lord to grow. I believe people can get spiritually apathetic by

---

[2] Earl D. Radmacher, Ronald B. Allen, and H. Wayne House, eds., *Nelson's New Illustrated Bible Commentary* (Nashville: Thomas Nelson, 1999), 1767.

[3] MacArthur, 2039.

[4] MacArthur, 2039.

soaking up His Word and then doing nothing with it. The *I AM* is "the Alpha and the Omega, the First and the Last, the Beginning and the End" (v. 13). As believers, we must stand up for the Word of God and for who Jesus is. The church is becoming soft when it does not stand up for the Lord. We must remember we have been forgiven by the blood of the Lamb and given access to the heavenly Father. We have been given eternal life, access to the tree of life, and can enter the city by the gates (v. 14). Our access to the Garden has been restored by God.

Revelation 22:15–21: Verse 15 states those who are immorally impure and of poor character will be left outside the gates. They are not walking with the Lord and will not get in. Verse 16 gives several titles for Jesus: the Root of David, the Offspring of David, and the Bright Morning Star. MacArthur explains, "Christ is the source (root) of David's life and line of descendants, which establishes His deity. He is also a descendant of David (offspring), which establishes His humanity."[5] MacArthur, also explains, the "Bright and Morning Star" is "the brightest star announcing the arrival of the day."[6] Jesus will be so bright that everything else will be illuminated by Him. In verse 17 both the Holy Spirit and the bride, which at this point includes the Old Testament saints as well as Jesus' followers, say "Come!" MacArthur shares, "This is an unlimited offer of grace and salvation to all who desire to have their thirsts quenched."[7] Verse 18 includes a warning to everyone not to add to the book of Revelation or God will punish them with the plagues described in the book. Verse 19 includes a warning not to take away from the prophecy of Revelation or God will take away eternal life. Revelation concludes with the reminder to testify that the Lord is coming quickly (v. 20). And then this closing: "The grace of the Lord Jesus be with all the saints. Amen."

Closing

Wiersbe states, "We must keep our lives clean" as we wait for Christ to return.[8] We have studied 66 books of the Bible in reviveSCHOOL to equip us to get ready for His return. I hope you're one step closer to being ready.

---

[5] MacArthur, 2040.

[6] MacArthur, 2040.

[7] MacArthur, 2040.

[8] Warren W. Wiersbe, *The Bible Exposition Commentary: Ephesians–Revelation* (Colorado Springs: David C. Cook, 1989), 614.

The Daily Word

As John's vision concluded, the Angel of the Lord affirmed the words spoken as faithful and true in order to show believers what must quickly take place before Christ returns. The one who keeps these prophetic words will be blessed. John began to worship the angel, but the angel insisted he stop and commanded John to only worship God. Believers will be made holy as they seek the Lord. By drinking the living water Jesus offers, no one will ever be thirsty again. Jesus promised He would come quickly. Jesus, the Great I Am, the Alpha and Omega, the Lord God Almighty, the Root, the Offspring of David, the Bright Morning Star is *coming quickly*. Until then, John prayed for Jesus' gift of grace to be with the saints.

You are living the final days before Christ's return. *Will you be ready?* Receive Christ's love for you. Live ready by keeping His Word. Love the Lord with all your heart, soul, mind, and strength. Then love others, as you love yourself. Worship God alone. Nothing else will ever satisfy you besides the love of Jesus. Christ is enough. Come, Lord Jesus, come. He is coming quickly. Be ready!

He who testifies about these things says, "Yes, I am coming quickly."
Amen! Come, Lord Jesus!
The grace of the Lord Jesus be with all the saints. Amen.
—Revelation 22:20–21

Further Scripture: Matthew 22:37–39; Ephesians 2:8–9; Revelation 22:7–9

Questions

1. Compare the beginning of creation to the final restoration in Revelation 22 (Genesis 1:5; 3:14–17, 24; Revelation 22:3, 5, 14).

2. What is the tree of life a symbol of (Genesis 2:9)? How does Revelation 22 describe the tree of life?

3. Why will there be no need for a lamp or even the sun in the New Jerusalem (John 8:12)?

4. Why should every believer study the book of Revelation (Revelation 1:3; 22:7)? Just like Matthew 5, the book of Revelation has some beatitudes. Find and read them (Revelation 1:3; 14:13; 16:15; 19:9; 20:6; 22:7, 14). How do these encourage you?

5. What does the book of Revelation imply by starting and ending the book with grace from the Lord Jesus (Ephesians 2: 8–9; Revelation1:4; 22:21)? How can you encourage someone with the words that you read in this book?

6. What did the Holy Spirit highlight to you in Revelation 22 through the reading or the teaching?

Contributing Authors

Dr. Kyle Lance Martin

Kyle Lance Martin is the founder of Time to Revive, a ministry based in Dallas, Texas, whose mission is to equip the saints for the return of Christ. His heart's desire, aside from loving his wife and four kids, is to engage people with the Word of God directly in their own environment. Kyle believes when people turn to the Messiah in humility and have a willingness to walk in the Holy Spirit, they can know and experience the calling of being a disciple of Jesus Christ. Kyle received his master of biblical studies from Dallas Theological Seminary and his doctor of ministry in outreach and discipleship from Gordon-Conwell Theological Seminary.

Pastor Gordon Henke

Gordon Henke is a pastor from northern Indiana, serving the church for 25 years. His passion is the studying of the Word. With confidence in the truth of the Word, he passionately helps people boldly share their faith.

Pastor Tom Schiefer

Tom Schiefer is the senior pastor of Nappanee First Brethren Church in Nappanee, Indiana. Prior to accepting a call to pastoral ministry, he was a band and choir director in Ohio. In the context of these two careers, he loves to orchestrate the Word of God, and the message it contains, into harmony with people's lives.

Pastor Fred Stayton

Fred Stayton is the lead pastor of Sonrise Church in Fort Wayne, Indiana, and has a passion for turning the hearts of fathers back to their children. Fred and his wife, Cheryl, have six children and one grandchild.

Ryan Schrag

Ryan Schrag is the national director for Time to Revive and has a heart to "equip the saints for the return of Christ" in the United States. Prior to joining full-time ministry, he was formerly the owner/operator of a lawn care business.

Wesley Morris

Wesley Morris is the Georgia state chairman for Time to Revive. A former construction worker turned pastor, he now trains and equips people to encounter Jesus and boldly share their faith.

Contributing Authors

Josh Edwards
Josh Edwards is the Minnesota state chairman for Time to Revive and leads worship both nationally and internationally. For the past 20 years he has been leading worship and speaking to the body of Christ about his heart's desire to see the church united, revived, and equipped to do the work of the ministry.

Shawn Carlson
Shawn Carlson is the executive director for Time to Revive. He has a strong desire to see people grow closer to Jesus through the study of God's Word and the carrying out of His mission.

Matt Reynolds
Matt Reynolds is the president of Spirit & Truth, a ministry aimed at equipping believers and churches to be more empowered by the Spirit, rooted in the truth, and mobilized for the mission. After serving as a local pastor for 13 years, Matt responded to a missionary calling to pursue Spirit-filled renewal in the church.

Larry Hopkins
Larry Hopkins is a businessman and entrepreneur in Dallas, Texas, who loves studying and discussing God's Word. He has a heart for revival, which stems from his love and desire for the Bible.

Pastor Kyle Felke
Kyle Felke is a former pastor in northern Indiana. He grew up in a home where both parents were teachers, which instilled in him a passion for teaching. This, combined with a love for Jesus, led him to pursue a biblical education and pastor a church in northern Indiana.

Contributing Authors

The Pentateuch
Kyle Lance Martin

The Gospels
Kyle Lance Martin
Josh Edwards
Ryan Schrag
Matt Reynolds

The Historical Books
Kyle Lance Martin
Wesley Morris
Josh Edwards
Pastor Gordon Henke
Pastor Tom Schiefer
Pastor Kyle Felke
Larry Hopkins

Acts
Kyle Lance Martin
Pastor Gordon Henke
Pastor Tom Schiefer
Wesley Morris
Shawn Carlson

The Wisdom Books
Kyle Lance Martin
Pastor Gordon Henke
Pastor Tom Schiefer
Wesley Morris
Ryan Schrag
Pastor Fred Stayton
Shawn Carlson
Josh Edwards

Paul's Letters
Kyle Lance Martin
Pastor Gordon Henke
Pastor Tom Schiefer
Wesley Morris
Shawn Carlson
Josh Edwards
Ryan Schrag

The Major Prophets
Kyle Lance Martin
Pastor Gordon Henke
Pastor Tom Schiefer
Pastor Fred Stayton
Ryan Schrag
Josh Edwards

General Letters
Kyle Lance Martin
Pastor Fred Stayton
Shawn Carlson

The Minor Prophets
Kyle Lance Martin
Josh Edwards

Revelation
Kyle Lance Martin
Pastor Gordon Henke
Pastor Tom Schiefer